Chorographia Britanniæ

THE
ENGLISH COUNTIES
Delineated by
THOMAS MOULE.

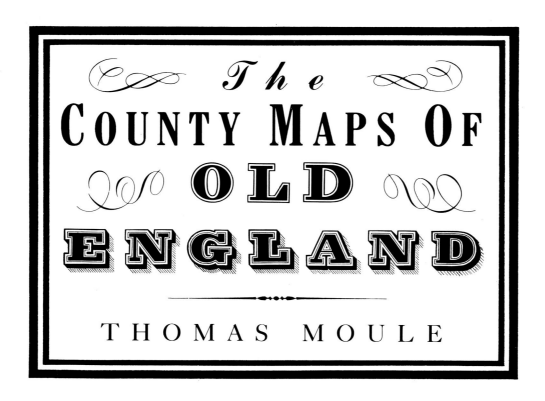

INTRODUCTION
BY

RODERICK BARRON

STUDIO EDITIONS
LONDON

Publisher's Note

This edition of Thomas Moule's County Maps
of England *is taken from maps that appeared in*
James Barclay's Complete and Universal
English Dictionary. *The maps have been*
coloured for this edition. The text is taken from
the county entries in this dictionary.

The County Maps of Old England
by Thomas Moule
Originally published in 1830 as
The English Counties Delineated

The text for this edition was
first published in
Barclay's Complete and Universal Dictionary, 1842

This edition published 1990 by Studio Editions Ltd.
Princess House, 50 Eastcastle Street
London W1N 7AP, England

Printed and bound in Spain

ISBN 1 85170 403 5

Contents

ENGLANDS

TOPOGRAPHER

or

MOULE'S ENGLISH COUNTIES

IN THE 19th CENTURY.

By

THOMAS MOULE.

Author of Bibliotheca Heraldica & Editor of several popular Topographical Works.

London,

Geo. Virtue, 26, Ivy Lane, Simpkin & Marshall, Stationers Court,

1836.

INTRODUCTION
By
RODERICK BARRON

Thomas Moule is one of the most distinctive and best-loved of early Victorian mapmakers. His charming series of English county maps, first published in 1830 as the *English Counties*, are as popular and collectable today as when they first appeared. Their elaborate and decorative style, a synthesis of art and cartography, sets them apart from most other maps of the period, whose plain unembellished style owed much to the pioneering work of the Ordnance Survey.

Moule's maps convey a picture of an England where 'ancientness' could still be found in abundance. This was an England where history was still alive in ancient country houses, parish churches with their escutcheoned Gothic memorials and tombs, in market towns and market places and in a landscape that still offered 'scenes, situations and prospects remarkable for extent and beauty' (*Prospectus*, 1830).

Yet the artistry and 'quaintness' of Moule's maps, more than any other mapmaker of the period, reflect his own interests as antiquary and author. They belie an England that was in fact in the throes of one of the greatest political, cultural and social upheavals it has ever experienced.

The 1830s, the decade in which Moule's maps first appeared, was one of the most politically and socially agitated of the century. In 1832 many believed England had come as close to revolution as at any stage in her history. As the Reform Bill of 1832 and Chartist riots and agitation of the 1830s swept away the idea of the graded, hierarchical agricultural community as the microcosm of the nation, England entered a new industrial age of change and uncertainty. The economic and social infrastructure of the nation was changed forever. New industries, such as textiles and iron, particularly in the North and Midlands, led to massive population movements from the country to the towns. Between 1821 and

1831 Liverpool grew by 46% and Manchester by some 40%. During the first half of the nineteenth century, London grew at a rate of 100,000 people per decade and was the hub of a new urban and industrialized world empire of over two million square miles and one hundred million people.

With such profound demographic and industrial changes came a communications revolution. The early nineteenth century, the great age of coach travel, saw a marked improvement in the turnpike network. Improvements in coach design, better roads and shorter stages (approximately ten miles) between horse changes made it possible to travel, for example, from York to London in under two days. In 1829 over 500 coaches covered some 12,000 miles of road and employed over 30,000 men and 150,000 horses.

The power of steam, which had transformed our industries, was soon harnessed to the transport system. The first commercial railway line, between Stockton and Darlington, was opened in 1825. Rapid expansion in the 1830s and 1840s produced a rail network of nearly 5000 miles. For the first time ever parts of the country which had hitherto been accessible only to the hardiest and most seasoned traveller came within the reach of even the most casual of 'tourists'. Rail travel held many attractions: fares in the 1840s were about half of equivalent coach fares; and the convenience of faster, safer and more commodious travel unleashed a completely new mass market of travellers. Some five million people travelled on the London to Birmingham line in 1839 – the year it opened – and an average of one million were using it annually by 1845. Add to this improvements in telegraphic communications and Rowland Hill's Penny Post letter service and we can see a picture of a new era of human mobility, where business and communications could be conducted with a speed and assurance hitherto unimaginable.

With the new industries came a new middle-class affluence and higher levels of education and literacy. Even before the Education Act of 1870 England had an unrivalled literacy rate of 80%. The availability of new cheap mass-circulation newspapers brought news and information to be disseminated among both the read and the unread. A mass market, mobile and relatively well-educated, provided a new impetus to the art of mapmaking. Early nineteenth-century England saw a new golden age of cartography comparable in certain respects to that of the seventeenth century.

For his attractive embellishments and richly decorative style Moule is often compared to his distinguished seventeenth-century predecessors, John Speed and Joan Blaeu. John Speed's *Theatre of the Empire of Great Britaine*, first published in 1611, and the English section of Joan Blaeu's *Atlas Novus* and *Atlas Maior*, published in the middle of the century, combined finely engraved topographical detail with vignette views, decorative cartouches and elaborate escutcheons, armorial bearings and coats of arms of the nobility and gentry of the counties depicted. Yet Moule and his contemporaries differed in a number of important ways.

Unlike his seventeenth- and eighteenth-century predecessor the early Victorian cartographer was no longer tied to the patronage of the aristocracy or the Crown, a patronage which in many cases had led to the debtor's prison. For pehaps the first time, atlases and their constituent maps were no longer expensive hand-produced items for the libraries of the wealthiest classes. Moule's avowed aim in the *English Counties* was 'to produce a work of obvious utility at a reasonable price, so as to place it within reach of every class' (Preface I iv). With this aim in mind Moule's maps were first published in parts at a price of 'ls plain or ls 6d coloured'. The industrial revolution made it possible to produce maps and atlases in greater numbers and at lower costs. The invention of the paper making machine and steam press were accompanied by improvements in the intaglio engraving process. Until the 1820s, copperplates were considered the most suitable medium for engraving, because of their softness and clarity. However, the long, highly skilled and laborious process was at best capable of producing only 200 impressions an hour: and because the plates were soft and easily worn down in printing they often required reworking and re-engraving after as few as 500 impressions.

The introduction of steel plates in the 1820s revolutionized the printing and appearance of maps. Because steel was harder and longer-lasting, longer printing runs were possible without reworking the plates. Steel also proved a more refined medium for the engraver. The process of heating and cooling the plates meant that finer lines could be etched closer together on the surface, allowing for more subtle variations in shading, definition and hachuring. Moule's maps are some of the finest examples of this new-found versatility and refinement.

Thomas Moule was born in the parish of Marylebone in 1784. Between 1816 and 1822 he carried on the business of bookseller in Duke Street, Grosvenor Square. Later he held the position of inspector of 'blind letters' (letters whose addresses were illegible or indecipherable) in the General Post Office. He simultaneously held the office of Chamber-keeper in the Lord Chamberlain's Office, which allowed him an official residence in the Stable Yard, St James's Palace, where he spent the later years of his life. He died in January 1851.

Clearly Moule was a man of many talents, combining commercial flair with a unique academic knowledge to which his long list of published works testifies.

In the space of thirty years he published works on the antiquities of Westminster Abbey, catalogues of books on heraldry and genealogy, a description of Elizabethan architecture and an essay on 'Roman Villas of the Augustan Age'. He also provided texts for the wide variety of illustrated plate books that emerged with advances in the printing process and steel plate engraving in the 1820s and 1830s. These included Westall's *Great Britain Illustrated* (1830), *The Illustrations of the Work of Walter Scott* (1834), and Winkle's *Cathedral Churches* and *Continental Cathedrals* (1836).

It was clearly Moule's intention to look back to the conservatism of the Middle Ages, almost as an escape from the upheavals of contemporary Victorian England. The price of England's industrialization had been high. The French observer Alexis de Tocqueville wrote of Manchester in his *Journeys to England and Ireland* (1835): 'From this foul drain the greatest stream of human industry flows out to fertilize the whole world. From this filthy sewer pure gold flows. Here humanity attains its most complete development and its most brutish; here civilization works its miracle and civilized man is turned back almost into a savage'.

One recurring feature of Moule's maps is their high Gothic style – numerous maps are set within Gothic pilasters, recesses and alcoves complete with armorial bearings and coats of arms. As an authority on the history of architecture Moule must have been aware of the great revival in Gothic architecture popularized by Auguste Pugin. This was a movement opposed to the new industrial and capitalistic age, a movement that looked back to the Middle Ages, to the roots of English society in its countryside and its history. It reached its climax in the year of Moule's death, 1851. At the Great Exhibition, within and yet juxtaposed with the very expression of the modern industrial age, the Crystal Palace, was Auguste Pugin's 'Medieval Court', a homely Gothic edifice harking back to an age of simplicity.

Looking at the illustrated works for which Moule supplied texts, it is clear that the direction of these new publications was to be the beauties of architecture and the landscape: cathedrals, churches, country houses on the one hand; the Alps, the Lake District, the Italian Lakes on the other. Walter Scott's works, for example, include many of the themes which inspired Moule himself – a fascination with the past and in bringing it alive, and a deep-seated interest in local history, local anecdotes and the beauties of the landscape.

In his *Prospectus*, accompanying the first separately issued part of the *English Counties*, the county of Berkshire (May 1830), Moule was clearly aware of the popular demand for these new works. He notes that works on local and provincial history, 'in the present state of national taste are regarded with increased attention'. Combing the works of the great antiquaries, he proposed to produce 'an interesting epitome of the Topographical History of the Kingdom'. His model, as he acknowledges in the Preface to the *Atlas* of 1836/7 was the Reverend Thomas Cox's early eighteenth-century history in six volumes, the *Magna Britannia* (1724). While he was ready to accommodate the modern traveller he was most concerned with describing those things closest to his heart. 'The admiration which the splendid remains of Antiquity now very generally excite, will render it desirable to point out all curious fragments of ancient architecture in monastic buildings, churches and crosses of religious foundation; all the Norman castles, the remains of feudal times; the castellated mansions of later date, and the Tudor houses of our nobility and gentry . . . nor will the more remote druidical circles, cromlechs, Roman and Danish barrows, tumuli etc. be entirely unnoticed.' Moule claims with great pride that in pursuit of this information he had, 'with expensive diligence personally visited every county in England excepting only Derbyshire and Cornwall' (Preface I iv).

What of the success of Moule's work? As we have said, the work first appeared in parts between 1830 and 1836, and each issue was accompanied by promising reviews from local newspapers. The maps, 'engraved purposely for this work, from the Best authorities, under the direction of eminent artists, will have every attention paid to render each as perfect as possible so as to combine accuracy with commodiousness of size and above all to obviate the inconvenience of folding'.

When first published in atlas form by George Virtue in 1837 as the *English Counties Delineated* (1837) it contained fifty-seven maps of England and Wales, of inland navigation, of the English counties and town plans of London, Bath, Boston, Portsmouth, Plymouth and the Isles of Thanet, Wight and Man. The engravers were among the foremost of the period – W. Schmollinger, John Dower and James Bingley. Between 1837 and 1839 the plates were frequently revised, the engravers' imprints often being changed and swapped around at the discretion of the publisher. The plates themselves required frequent revision due to two important factors – the Reform Bill of 1832 and the expanding railway network. The Reform Bill led to a redistribution of parliamentary seats, disenfranchising the antiquated system of pocket and rotten boroughs and recognizing the emergence of the new urban towns. Information on the new constituences and the number of MPs returned to Parliament were added to the maps. At the same time the rapid expansion of the new rail network necessitated repeated updating. The new mass market of railway travellers posed immediate problems for mapmakers such as Moule; Maps became obsolete as soon as they were engraved. Virtue seemed to care little, issuing both old stock and new revised maps simultaneously.

Moule's maps found a greater audience when they were issued to accompany the 'Complete and Universal English Dictionary by the Reverend James Barclay . . . Revised by Henry W. Dewhurst Esq. F.E.S.L.', editions of which appeared between 1842 and 1852. In the philanthropic tradition of mid-Victorian England, the aim of the dictionary was to provide a compendium of information for the education and enlightenment of those who had neither means nor hope of even the most basic education.

The maps also found popularization in the 1870s, often being found bound into copies of *The History of England* by Hume and Smollett, though only some thirty of the county maps appeared in this series.

Clearly Virtue the publisher was aware of the lasting popularity of Moule's maps. Their life-span of over forty years was much longer than almost any other series of Victorian maps.

In a modern society haunted by the spectres of industrialism, urban decline and environmental destruction, we can, like the early Victorian, appreciate Thomas Moule's maps for their old-fashioned quaintness and artistry. It is these qualities which, without a doubt, account for their continued popularity with map collectors.

Moule's maps constitute one of the finest visual records of the profound changes of early nineteenth-century England when, on the framework of an ancient, almost timeless, county landscape, were being laid the bones of a new age of industrialism and democracy. Moule struck a chord not only with the Victorian of this new industrial age but with scholars and collectors of every generation since.

THE MAPS

Great Britain

The principal of the British Isles, and the largest island of Europe. It lies to the north west of that continent, and is divided from it by the English Channel, the Straits of Dover, the German Ocean, and the North Sea. It is about 600 miles in length, and from 100 to 300 miles in breadth. Its chief capes are, Land's End and Lizard Point, Start Point, Dungeness, North Foreland, Spurn Head and Flamborough Head, Cape Wrath, the Mull of Cantire, the Mull of Galloway, St. David's Head, and Hartland Point. The Wash, the Friths of Forth, Moray, and Dornoch, those of Pentland, Clyde, and Solway, the Minch, the North Channel, the Irish Sea and St. George's Channel between it and Ireland, Caernarvon and Cardigan Bays, the Bristol Channel, Mount's Bay, and Torbay, are the chief gulfs and bays around it. The north and west parts of the island (Scotland and Wales) are mountainous, and there are rocky elevations in Cumberland and Cornwall; the rest of the surface is broken by fine sweeping ranges of hills. The loftiest points in Scotland are about 4000 feet high, those in Wales, about 3500, those in Cumberland are about the same height: the Derbyshire hills have points nearly 2000 feet in height, and the chalk hills range below 1000. The chief rivers are the Thames, the Severn, the Ouse, the Trent, the Humber, the Forth, the Tay, and the Clyde. It possesses every variety of scenery, and abounds especially in rich rural and woodland prospects. Its mineral wealth is considerable: iron and tin, with other metals less abundant; coal; limestone, and all kinds of building-stone; have made it independent of other countries for those invaluable productions. It has also salt-mines, and mineral springs. But its agricultural advantages are equally great; it has soils naturally adapted to every variety of growth, and capable, with judicious and scientific culture, of yielding most copiously; and all kinds of pasture land, from the high sheep-walks of the wolds, to the rich low meadows suited for other cattle. Its manufactures embrace every kind of necessary for man, and have long been looked at as the most extensive and the best in the world. These have been the chief stay of its commerce, which embraces every spot inhabited by civilized man, and many of those tenanted by the rudest nations of the globe. Its climate is proverbially fickle, and yet it knows none of the severe atmospheric pests of other climes, and its people are healthy and strong in spite of all disadvantages. It has not a single noxious wild animal, and no poisonous reptile, save the viper, which is by no means common. Such advantages, rendered secure by its insular position, compensate for its manifold wants, most of which commerce supplies, and make it a spot which might be rendered one of the most favoured on the earth. It has, beside small islands, the Isles of Wight and of Man, Anglesea, Arran and Bute, Islay, &c., the Western Isles and Skye, the Orkneys and the Shetland Isles, lying in various directions around it. Population, including these islands, 18,844,434.

England and Wales

England is the southern and most considerable portion of the island of Great Britain, so named after the most numerous of the Saxon tribes who, in the 5th and 6th centuries, took possession of it. It is surrounded on the east, south and west by the German Ocean, the English Channel, and the Irish Sea; to the north of it lies Scotland, and about the middle of the west side, Wales. It is about 350 miles in length, and 200 in breadth in the midland district. It is divided into 40 counties, or shires, of which Yorkshire is the largest and Rutland the smallest; and these are divided into ridings, hundreds, rapes, wapentakes, and other smaller divisions, for civil legislation. Ecclesiastically, it is divided into two provinces, Canterbury and York; and these are subdivided into twenty-six bishoprics, under which are deaneries, archdeaconries, and parishes.

Wales is a principality of England. It lies on the Irish Sea, with St. George's Channel and Bristol Channel on the south, and it is bounded by the counties of Chester, Salop, Hereford, and Monmouth. It is about 180 miles long, and 60 in mean breadth. It comprehends 12 counties; namely, Anglesey, Caernarvonshire, Denbighshire, Flintshire, Merionethshire, and Montgomeryshire, in North Wales; Brecknockshire, Cardiganshire, Caermarthenshire, Glamorganshire, Pembrokeshire, and Radnorshire, in South Wales; and contains 751 parishes, and 58 market towns. The country is very mountainous, and abounds with iron, copper, lead, and coal mines, with quarries of free-stone, slate, &c. &c. Some of its mountains exceed 3000 feet in height. Snowdon and Plinlimmon are the most celebrated. It is watered with many rivers, of which the principal are the Dee, Wye, Usk, Conway, Cluyde, and Towy. Corn and the usual agricultural produce of the island are abundant. Its fisheries are good, but its manufactures are not considerable. It has some fine ports and harbours, and a good trade. It returns 29 members to parliament. Population, 911,321. It gives the title to the eldest son of the reigning monarch of Great Britain.

ENGLAND
AND
WALES.

ENGLISH MILES
10 20 30 40 50 60

Bedfordshire

A county in England, about 36 miles in length, and 22 in breadth. It contains 9 hundreds, 10 market towns, 124 parishes, and 107,936 inhabitants, and sends four members to parliament. The Ouse and the Ivel are its chief streams; and the Lea has its source here. The great range of chalk hills passes through this county, whence it arises that it is more noted for pastures, than for arable or wood land. It is a pleasant inland county, and diversified with fruitful plains and rising hills, abounding in cattle, corn, and rich pastures; it is noted for barley, bone lace, and a manufacture of straw goods.

BEDFORD

It is seated on the river Ouse, which divides it into two parts, united by a bridge with two gates, one at each end, to stop the passage occasionally. It has five churches, of which St. Paul's is a very noble building, and formerly had a strong castle. The charitable institutions are very numerous, and the lunatic asylum, the infirmary, the grammar school, and some others are handsome buildings. Markets, Monday, for pigs; Saturday, for corn, &c. 50 miles from London. Population, 9178.

WOBURN

It is a neat town, with some good buildings; and was formerly famous for its abbey, which now belongs to the Duke of Bedford, and is his country seat. Near it is found great plenty of fullers' earth. It is 42 miles from London. Market, Friday. Population, 1914.

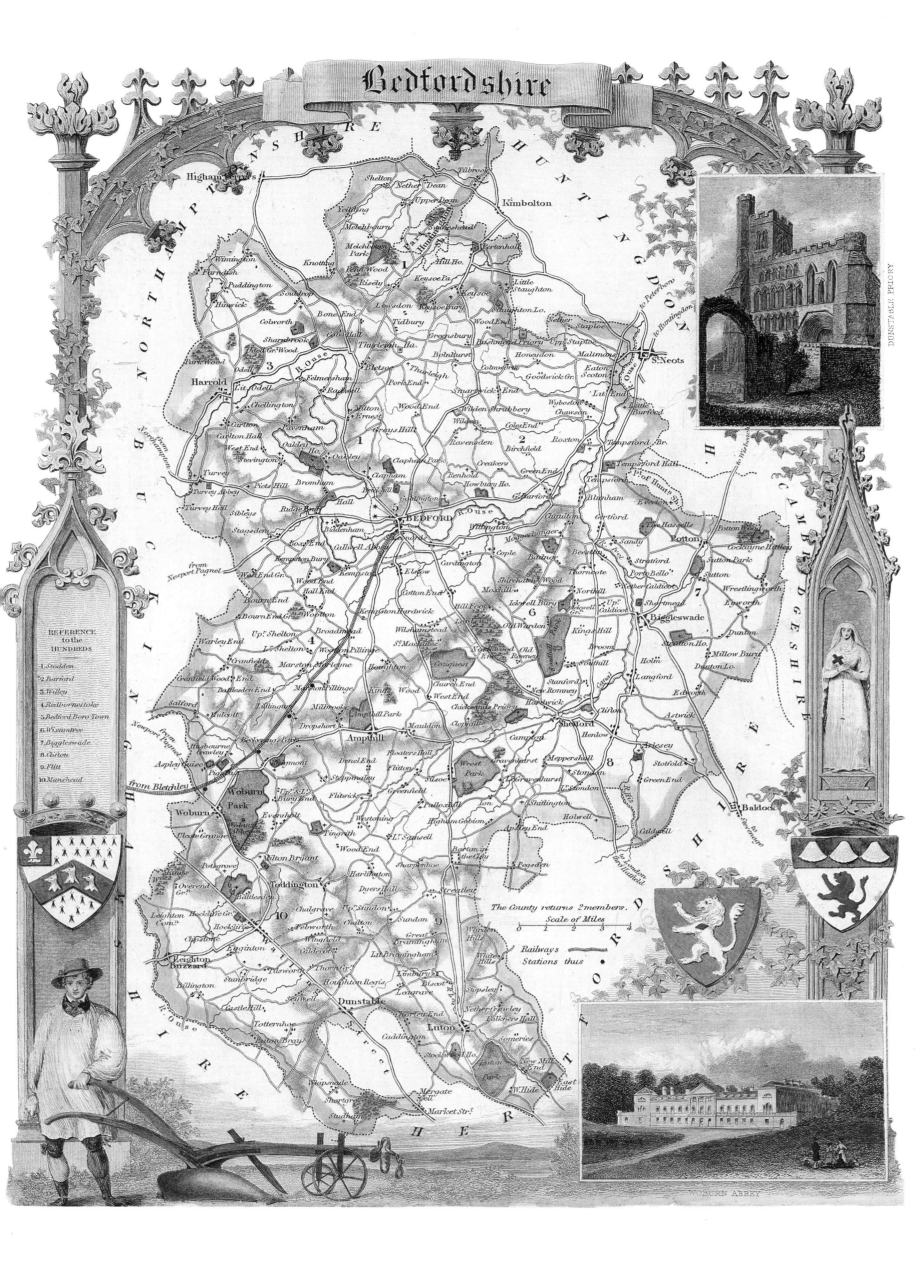

Bedfordshire

DUNSTABLE PRIORY

WOBURN ABBEY

REFERENCE to the
HUNDREDS

1. Stodden
2. Barford
3. Willey
4. Redbornestoke
5. Bedford Boro Town
6. Wixamtree
7. Biggleswade
8. Flitton
9. Flitt
10. Manshead

The County returns 2 members.

Scale of Miles
0 1 2 3 4

Railways
Stations thus

Berkshire

A county of England, bounded on the north by Oxfordshire and Buckinghamshire, on the west by Wiltshire, on the south by Hampshire and Surrey, and on the east by Middlesex and Buckinghamshire. It is about 40 miles long, and 25 broad. The great chalk range, which reaches, at the White Horse Hill, nearly 900 feet in height, runs nearly due west through it. It has good pastures on these hills, and the lower land is fertile and woody. The Thames is its chief river; it has also the Kennet, the Loddon, the Auburn, &c. It is mainly an agricultural county; but some woollen cloth is manufactured. The White Horse Hill and Vale are named so from the figure of a horse rudely made on the side of the chalk hill by cutting away the turf from the chalk below; it is nearly 400 feet long, and may be seen for many miles, and is believed to be of great antiquity. Reading, Abingdon, Windsor, Wallingford, &c., are its chief towns. It returns nine members to parliament. Population, 161,147.

Reading

It is pleasantly seated on the river Kennet, near its confluence with the Thames, and has several bridges. The newer parts of the town are tolerably well built, and there are several public edifices, which greatly ornament it. It has also some interesting ruins. It has a good trade, possessing several valuable manufactures, beside being an emporium for corn, malt, &c. It has also by canal and railroad great facilities for the transport of its commodities. It is 39 miles from London. Markets, Saturday (for corn), and Monday (for cattle). Fairs, February 2, May 1, July 25, and September 21. Population, 18,937.

Windsor

It is pleasantly seated on the banks of the Thames, in a healthful air, and is a handsome, large and well-inhabited place; but chiefly famous for its magnificent castle, which is a royal palace, and is surrounded by a fine park, in which is the beautiful artificial lake, called Virginia Water. It is 22 miles from London. Market, Saturday. Population, 7528; of Old Windsor, 1600.

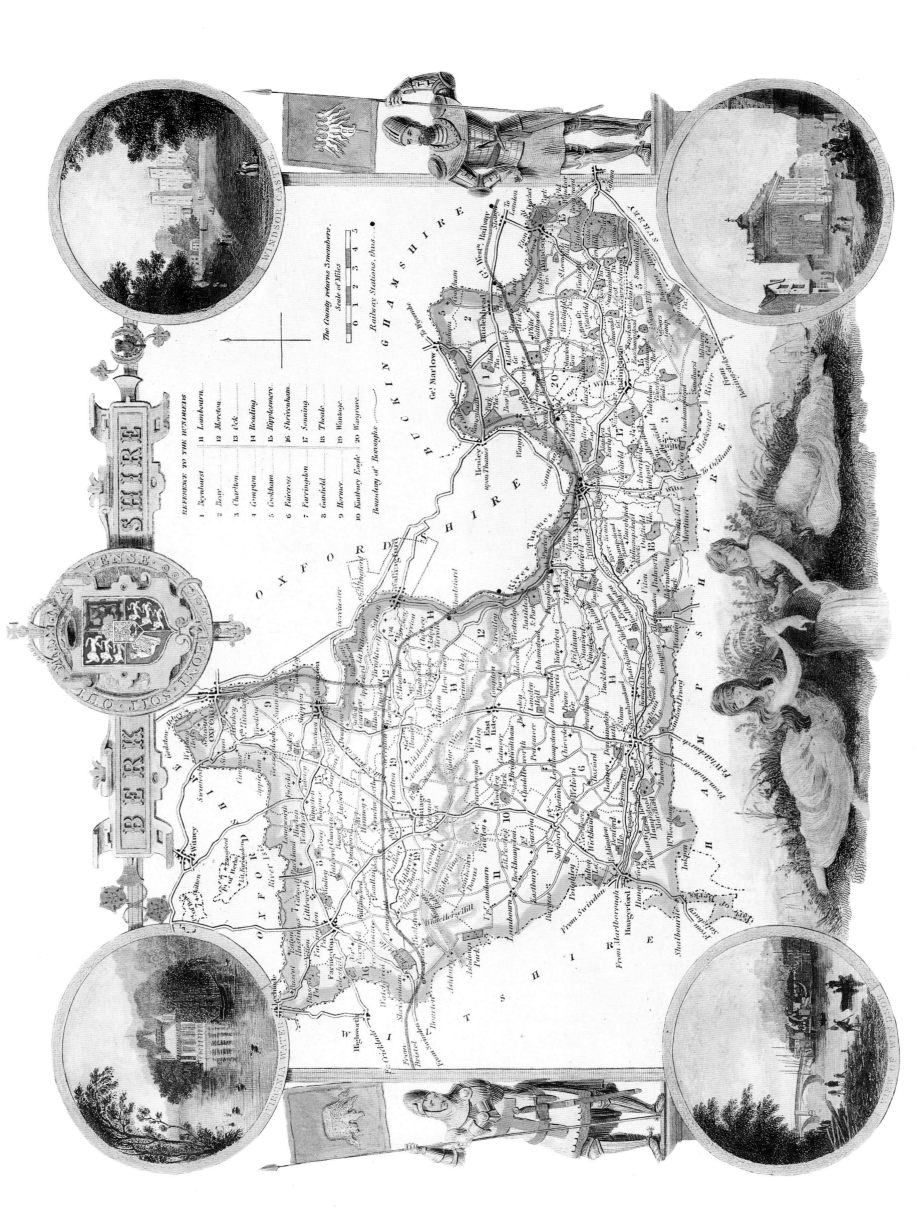

BERKSHIRE

HONI SOIT QUI MAL Y PENSE.

The County returns 3 members.

Scale of Miles

0 1 2 3 4 5

Railway Stations, thus

REFERENCE TO THE HUNDREDS

1 Kenbury   11 Lambourn
2 Bray   12 Moreton
3 Charlton   13 Ock
4 Compton   14 Reading
5 Cookham   15 Ripplesmore
6 Faircross   16 Shrivenham
7 Farringdon   17 Soning
8 Ganfield   18 Theale
9 Hormer   19 Wantage
10 Kintbury Eagle   20 Wargrave

Boundary of Boroughs

WINDSOR CASTLE

VIRTUTIS WATER

OXFORDSHIRE

BUCKINGHAMSHIRE

SURREY

HAMPSHIRE

WILTSHIRE

River Thames

Buckinghamshire

A county of England, bounded on the north by Northamptonshire, on the east by Bedfordshire, Hertfordshire, and Middlesex, on the west by Oxfordshire, and on the south by Berkshire, from which it is separated by the river Thames. It is about 50 miles in length, and 18 in breadth. The great range of chalk hills, called the Chilterns, runs through the county, and attains an elevation of more than 900 feet above the level of the sea. On one side of this range flow the Thames, the Thame, and the Colne; and on the other the Ouse. The soil is variable, but in some parts it is very rich. The air is mild, and the county reckoned in general healthy. By means of canals and railroad it has every facility for trade. But its productions are almost wholly pastoral and agricultural. It returns 11 members to parliament. Population, 155,983.

Buckingham

It is situated on a low ground, on the river Ouse, by which it is almost surrounded, and over it are three handsome stone bridges. There was formerly a strong castle in the middle of the town. There is a county jail, and a town-hall. It has but one church. It is 57 miles from London. Market, Saturday. Population, 4054.

Chiltern

A chain of chalky hills, separating the counties of Bedford and Hertford, and running through the middle of Buckinghamshire, from Tring, Hertfordshire, to Henley upon Thames, Oxfordshire. They are covered, in various parts, with woods, and some of the eminences are of considerable height, and afford rich prospects. To these hills is annexed the nominal office of steward under the crown, the acceptance of which, of consequence, enables a member of the British parliament to vacate his seat.

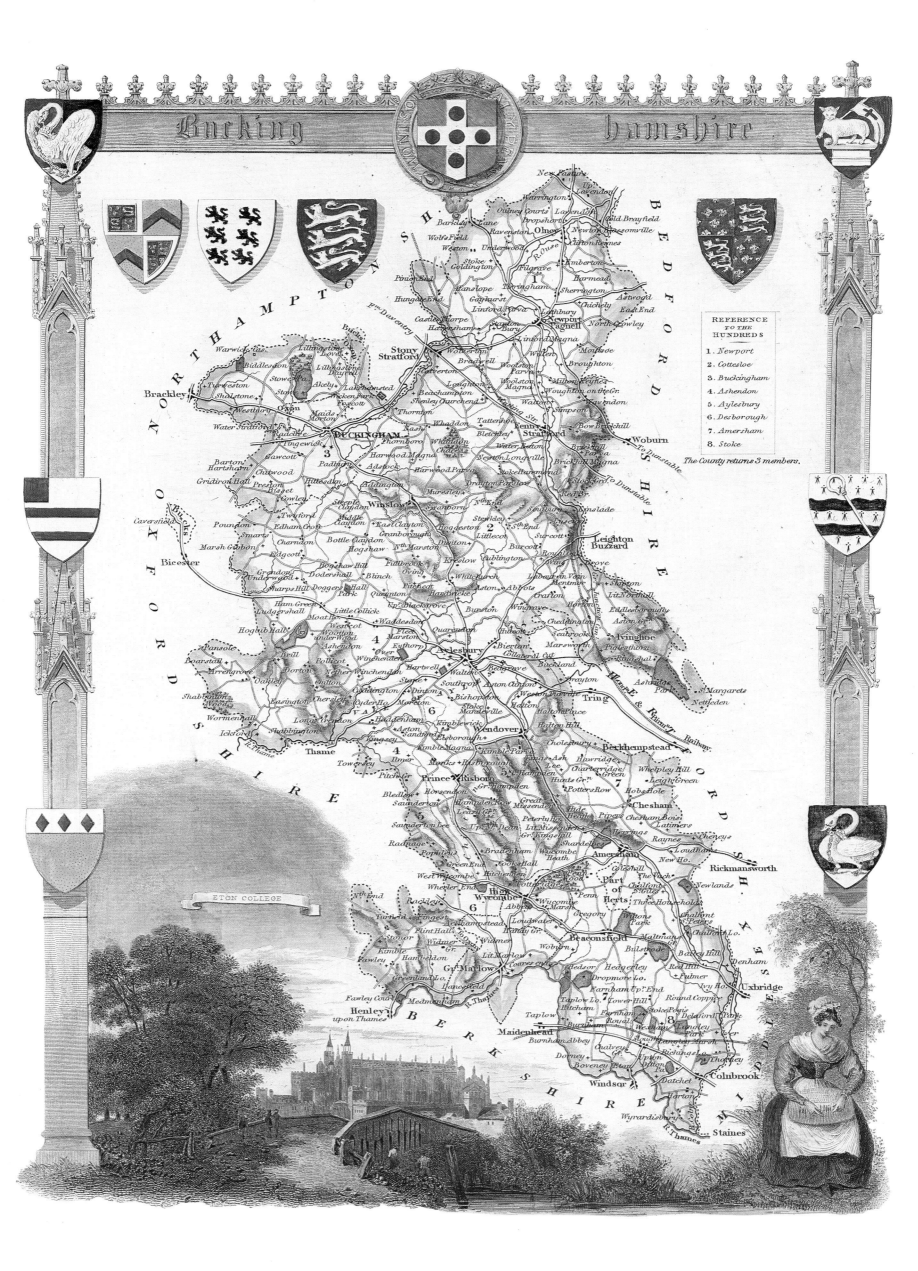

Buckinghamshire

REFERENCE
TO THE
HUNDREDS

1. Newport
2. Cottesloe
3. Buckingham
4. Ashendon
5. Aylesbury
6. Desborough
7. Amersham
8. Stoke

The County returns 3 members.

ETON COLLEGE

Cambridgeshire

A county of England, bounded by the counties of Bedford, Huntingdon, Northampton, Lincoln, Norfolk, Suffolk, Essex, and Hertford. It is 50 miles in length from north to south, and 25 broad from east to west. The air and soil vary; the south and east parts are pleasant and healthy, but the north or fenny country is low and watery. The Nen and Ouse, the Cam, and the Larke, are its rivers; and the only hills of any note are the trifling elevations called the Gogmagog Hills. It is an agricultural county, and not unproductive. Population, 164,459. It returns seven members to parliament.

Bedford Level

The name of the vast expanse of marshland lying between the counties of Norfolk, Suffolk, Cambridge, Huntingdon, Northampton, and Lincoln, and the sea. It was during the reigns of the Saxon monarchs of England a tidal estuary, with one or two fertile islands, surrounded by the sea at high water, and by broad rivers with immense banks of mud at low water and crossed by one or two Roman roads on embankments. At the Conquest it was so far laid dry, that many of the Saxons retreated to it, as the last security from the Normans, and here the camp of refuge was formed. In the 15th century the feasibility of draining this barren and pestilential tract was discussed; various attempts were subsequently made, the most successful being in the troublous times of the 17th century, by Francis, Earl of Bedford; from whom it is named. The drainage may now be regarded as almost complete, and by a wonderful combination of embankments, dikes, new river-courses, with locks, and draining mills, many thousands of acres have been reclaimed, and added to the pasture and arable land of the country.

Ely

It has but one good street, well paved, the rest being unpaved, and miserably dirty. The minster is a fine building, and has a stately tower, which can be seen at a great distance. The bishops have all the rights of Counts Palatine, which also they had through the whole Isle of Ely, till the reign of Henry VIII. Ely is completely subordinate to the bishop in its civil government, and is the only city in England unrepresented in parliament. It has become a central railway station, which may be expected to rub off a little of its medieval rust soon. It is seated on a rising ground, near the river Ouse and other streams, the former of which is navigable to Lynn, and by which it carries on a pretty good trade. It is 66 miles from London. Market, Saturday. Population, 6825.

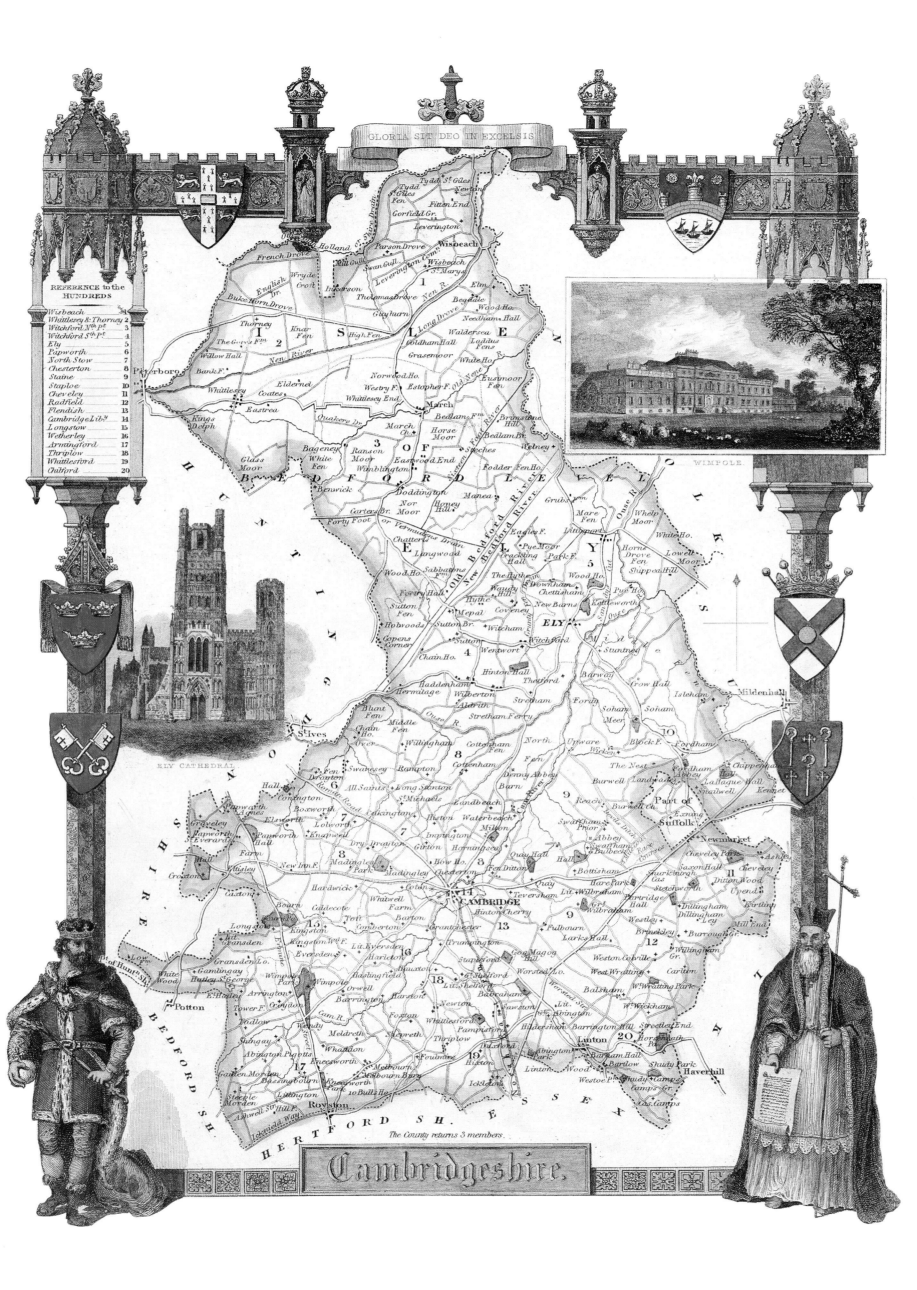

GLORIA SIT DEO IN EXCELSIS

REFERENCE to the
HUNDREDS

Wisbeach	1
Whittlesey & Thorney	2
Witchford N⁰.P⁺.	3
Witchford S⁰.P⁺.	4
Ely	5
Papworth	6
North Stow	7
Chesterton	8
Staine	9
Staploe	10
Cheveley	11
Radfield	12
Flendish	13
Cambridge Lib⁴	14
Longstow	15
Wetherley	16
Armingford	17
Thriplow	18
Whittlesford	19
Chilford	20

WIMPOLE

ELY CATHEDRAL

Cambridgeshire.

The County returns 3 members.

Cambridge

It is the county town and seat of a celebrated university, and is seated on the river Cam, which divides it into two unequal parts. The university contains 13 colleges and 4 halls. Its buildings are elegant, and its libraries and cabinets valuable and extensive. The Fitzwilliam Museum, Senate House, Observatory, &c., are connected with it. The town-hall and county-hall are the only buildings of note that do not appertain to the university. The streets are narrow, but well paved, and the houses are old; the market-place is spacious, and in it is a handsome stone conduit, to which water is conveyed by an aqueduct. It communicates with London and the north by railway. It is 51 miles from London. Markets every day in the week, Sunday and Monday excepted. Population, 24,453.

TRINITY COLLEGE

A college at Cambridge, founded in the 16th century, on the bases of two earlier colleges, which had lapsed to the king. It takes the lead in the university, and has very spacious buildings, and a library built by Wren. It is very wealthy, and has produced many great scholars.

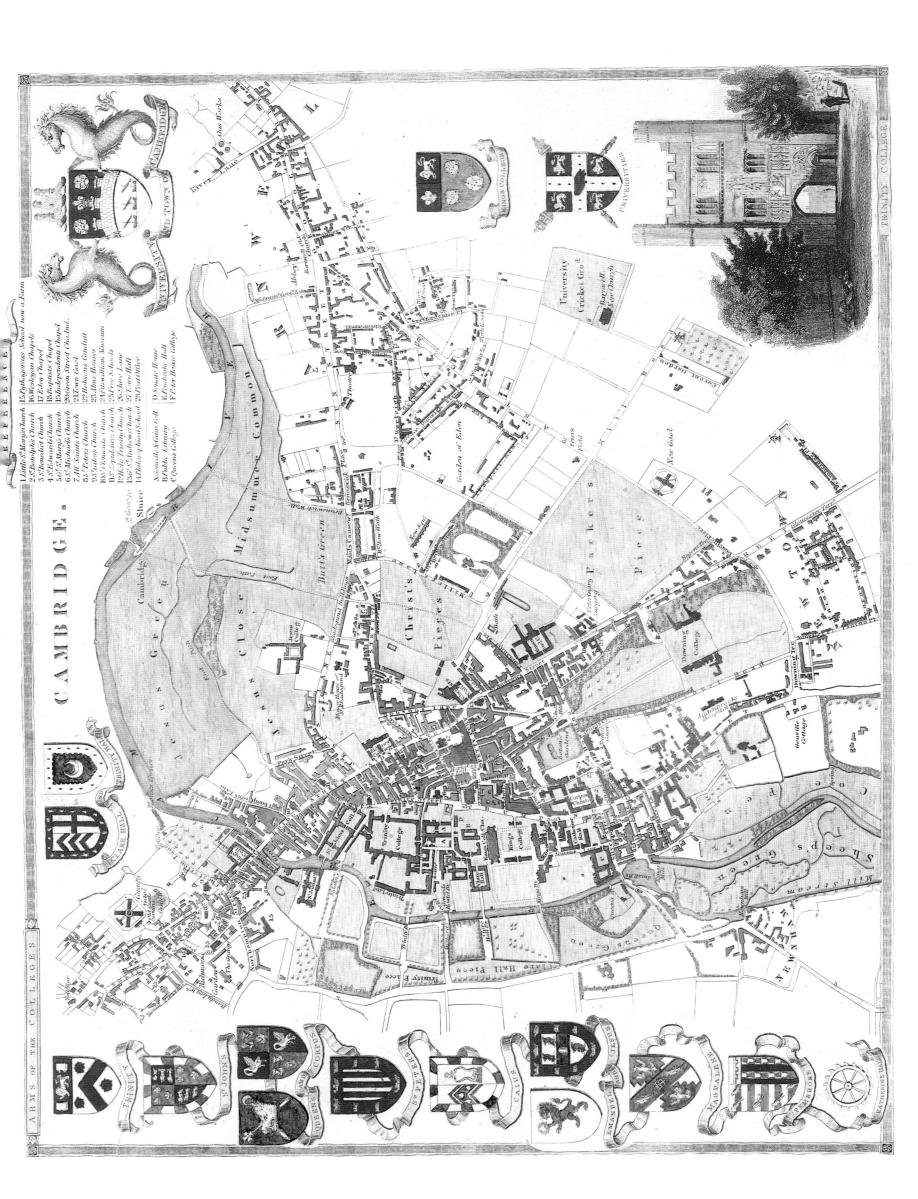

CAMBRIDGE.

Cheshire

A county Palatine of England, lying on the Irish Sea, and bounded by Lancashire, Yorkshire, Derbyshire, Staffordshire, Shropshire, and Wales. It is about 60 miles in length, and 30 in breadth. The surface is generally even, but it has some hills. It is watered by the Mersey, the Dee, and the Weaver, with their lesser tributary streams. It has also some great canals, and railroads, as means of communication. Coal and rock-salt, with some useful kinds of sandstone, are found here; and the salt is a very prominent feature in the wealth of the county. Dairy-farming is extensively pursued, and much cheese produced. There are some manufactures in this county, principally on the borders of Lancashire, of cotton, silk, woollens, &c. &c. And these, with its salt and its cheese, are its exports, not only to other parts of the kingdom, but all over the world. It has 101 parishes. Besides its rivers, there are many good-sized lakes in this county. It is also famed for its forests and plantations. Its population is 395,660. Chester is the county town.

CHESTER

A large and ancient city, seated on the Dee, over which there is a noble bridge, by which vessels come from the sea to the quay; and having, by a canal, communication with most of the inland navigations. The main streets are hollowed out in the rock to a considerable depth, and the houses have, elevated in front, covered porticoes, which are called rows, and afford a sheltered way for foot passengers. The city has four gates and three posterns, and is 2 miles in compass. It consists chiefly of four large streets, which are pretty even and spacious, and as they cross one another in straight lines, meeting in the centre, they make an exact cross, with the town-house or exchange, a neat structure, near the middle. In the old castle, where the Earls of Chester formerly held their parliaments, was a stately hall, somewhat like that at Westminster, where the Palantine courts and assizes were held, before the erection of the new prison. It has nine well-built churches, and a cathedral, dedicated to St. Werburgh, which is very ancient. Chester has a manufactory of gloves and tobacco-pipes, and a considerable traffic of shop goods into North Wales. It has also a constant communication with Ireland. It is 181 miles from London. Markets, Wednesday and Saturday. Population, 23,115.

DEE

A river of North Wales and Cheshire, which rises near Pimble Meer, in Merionethshire, crosses the county of Denbigh, separating it from Cheshire, and runs into the Irish Channel, about 15 miles north west of Chester, and to which city is navigable from near Ellesmere in Shropshire.

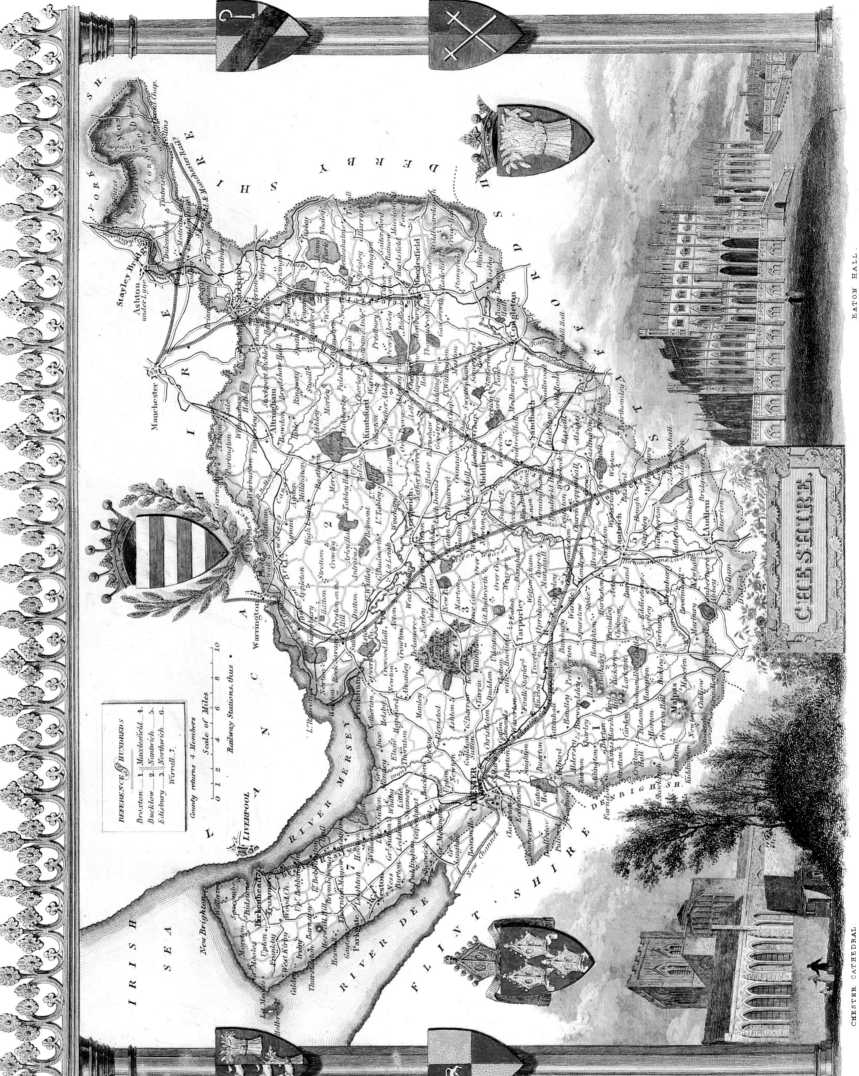

CHESTER CATHEDRAL.

EATON HALL.

CHESHIRE.

REFERENCES to HUNDREDS

Broxton . . 1. Macclesfield 4.
Bucklow . . 2. Nantwich . 5.
Eddisbury . 3. Northwich . 6.
             Wirrall . 7.

County returns 4 Members

Scale of Miles

Railway Stations, thus

Cornwall

A county of England, which forms the south west extremity of Great Britain. It is bounded on the east by Devonshire; its other parts are washed by the sea. Its length from east to west is 74 miles, and its greatest breadth about 43; on the south west it terminates in two promontories, the Lizard Point and the Land's End. It contains 9 hundreds, and 206 parishes. The central part, which is the highest, is mostly covered with barren moors, but there are fertile tracts beside the rivers which flow to the north and south of it. The Tamar, the Camel, the Fowey, the Fal, &c. are its chief streams. Its being surrounded on three sides by the sea, keeps its temperature very even, there being seldom any severe frosts, or great heats, and spring being earlier here than in the rest of England; but it is exposed to storms, and has abundance of rainy and foggy weather. Its chief importance arises from its mineral riches. It has valuable copper mines, in which gold and silver are sometimes met with in small quantities. Its tin mines are most extensive, and celebrated in remotest antiquity. Lead, iron, zinc, arsenic &c., also occur. There are very many kinds of rock quarried here, for building, as granite and freestone, slates for roofing, grit for making millstones, &c. A species of very clear crystal is common, which is known to jewellers as the Cornish diamond. The growth of corn is not considerable for its extent, nor the numbers of cattle. It was one of the retreats of the ancient Britons when the Saxons seized the east parts of the island, and it is but lately that the last remnant of the old Celtic dialect of this island has become extinct. It gives a ducal title to the eldest son of the sovereign; and as revenue, he has the proceeds of a duty charged on all the tin raised. Launceston and Bodmin are its two chief towns. Population, 341,279. It returns 14 members to parliament.

BODMIN

It is seated in a bottom between two high hills, which renders the air very unwholesome. It chiefly consists of one street, and the many decayed houses show it has been a place of greater note; it formerly had the privilege of the coinage of tin. It is 334 miles from London. Market, Saturday. Population, 4643.

LAUNCESTON

It had formerly a monastery, and a noble castle, because of its strength called Castle Terrible, the lower part of which is now made use of for the jail. It is seated on the river Tamar. It is 214 miles from London. Markets, Thursday and Saturday. Population, 2460.

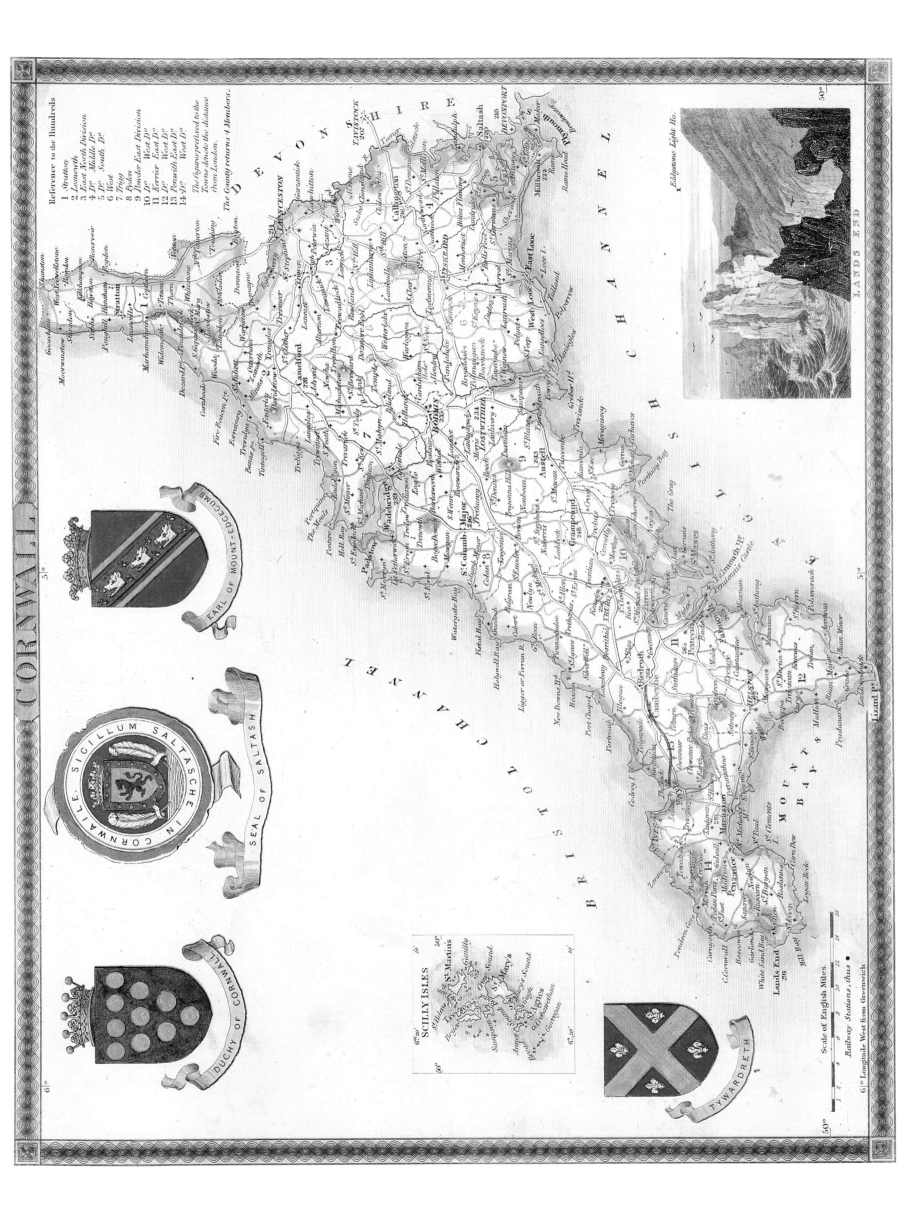

CORNWALL

Reference to the Hundreds
1 Stratton
2 Lesnewth
3 East North Division
4 Dº Middle Dº
5 Dº South Dº
6 West
7 Trigg
8 Pyder
9 Powder East Division
10 Dº West Dº
11 Kerrier East Dº
12 Dº West Dº
13 Penwith East Dº
14 Dº West Dº

The figures prefixed to the
Towns denote the distance
from London.
The County returns 4 Members.

EARL OF MOUNT-EDGECUMB

SIGILLUM SALTASCHE IN CORNWAILE.

SEAL OF SALTASH

DUCHY OF CORNWALL

TYWARDRETH

SCILLY ISLES

Eddystone Light Ho.

LANDS END

Scale of English Miles.

Railway Stations, thus •

6° Longitude West from Greenwich

Cumberland

A maritime county of England, bounded on the west by the Irish Sea and Solway Frith; on the north by Scotland; on the east by Northumberland, Durham, and Westmoreland; and on the south west and south by the sea and Lancashire. It is 58 miles in length, and its greatest breadth is about 45 miles. All but the north part of this county is very hilly, or even mountainous, Helvellyn, Skiddaw, Cross-Fell, and some other heights exceeding 3000 feet. Amidst these mountains and hills are lakes, of no great extent, but of most romantic beauty. Its streams are the Eden, the Derwent, the Esk, &c., some of which have in their course several noble waterfalls. There are mines of lead, copper, iron, and even of silver; but those of black-lead, or plumbago, are the most peculiar. Coal, slate, limestone, granite, and various building-stones, also occur in various degrees of abundance. There is good pasturage even among the hills, and the arable land is fertile. It contains 1 city, 2 boroughs, 17 market towns. Carlisle is the county town. Population, 178,038. It returns 9 representatives to parliament.

CARLISLE

It is pleasantly situated on a rising ground, in a fertile country, near the confluence of 3 fine rivers, the Eden, the Peterell, and the Cauda, or Caude, all abounding with fish, and by which it is nearly surrounded. It has long been noted for making whips and fish-hooks; there are also considerable quantities of printed linens, checks, cottons, fustians, hats, tanned leather, nails, coarse knives, stockings, &c., manufactured here. It is 301 miles from London. Markets, Wednesday and Saturday. Population, 23,012.

DERWENT-WATER

The name of one of the most beautiful lakes of Cumberland, 3 miles in length, and about a mile and a half in breadth. In this lake is seen the floating island, of which so many different accounts have been given by natural philosophers. It abounds with fish, and there are fine salmon in the season.

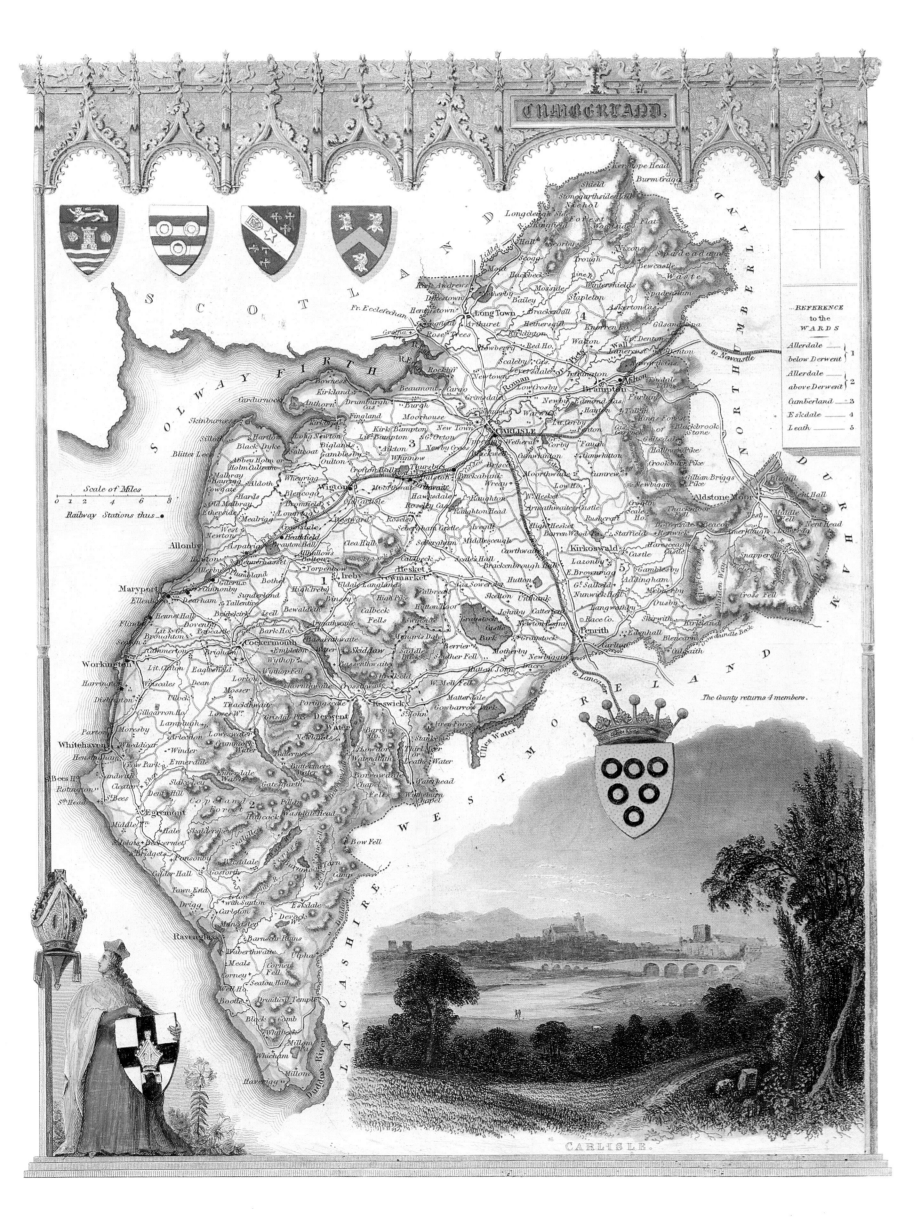

CUMBERLAND.

CARLISLE.

REFERENCE
to the
WARDS

Allerdale
below Derwent } 1
Allerdale
above Derwent } 2
Cumberland ——— 3
Eskdale ——— 4
Leath ——— 5

The County returns 4 members.

Scale of Miles
0 1 2 4 6 8
Railway Stations thus ⋯

SCOTLAND

SOLWAY FIRTH

NORTHUMBERLAND

DURHAM

WESTMORELAND

LANCASHIRE

Derbyshire

A county of England, bounded by Cheshire, Staffordshire, Yorkshire, Nottinghamshire, Leicestershire, and Warwickshire. It extends nearly 56 miles in length from north to south, and 34 from east to west where broadest; but in the south part it is not above six. It is divided into six hundreds. The north and west parts are mountainous, some heights being nearly 2000 feet above the sea. The south and east parts are fertile, producing most kinds of grain, particularly barley. The mountains abound in the best lead, with marble, alabaster, mill-stones, iron, coal, and a coarse sort of crystal. There is good pasture in the valleys. Some important manufactures are carried on in this county. The principal rivers are the Derwent, Dove, Erwash, and Trent. It returns six members to parliament. Population, 272,217.

DERBY

It is a large and well-built town, with a spacious market-place and handsome town-house. Here are manufactories of silk, cotton, and worsted stockings, and of elegant porcelain, which last is in high estimation. Derbyshire and foreign marbles are wrought here in vases, urns, columns, and other ornamental articles, and the lapidary and jewellery branches are executed with great neatness. Malting and earthenware-making are also carried on here. It is seated on the river Derwent, which is navigable to the Trent. It is 120 miles from London. Markets, Wednesday and Friday. Population, 32,741.

DERWENT

A river of Derbyshire, which rises in the High Peak, and passing through the county, falls into the Trent, 8 miles from Derby. Also, a river of Yorkshire, which rises in the North Riding, and running south falls into the Ouse, 5 miles south east of Selby. Also, a river of Durham, flowing through a romantic tract of county, and falling into the Tyne, a little above Newcastle, near which, on its banks, are some capital iron works. Also, a river of Cumberland, which rises in Borrowdale, and flowing through Derwent-Water and Bassingthwaite-Water, passes by Cockermouth, and falls into the Irish Sea at Workington.

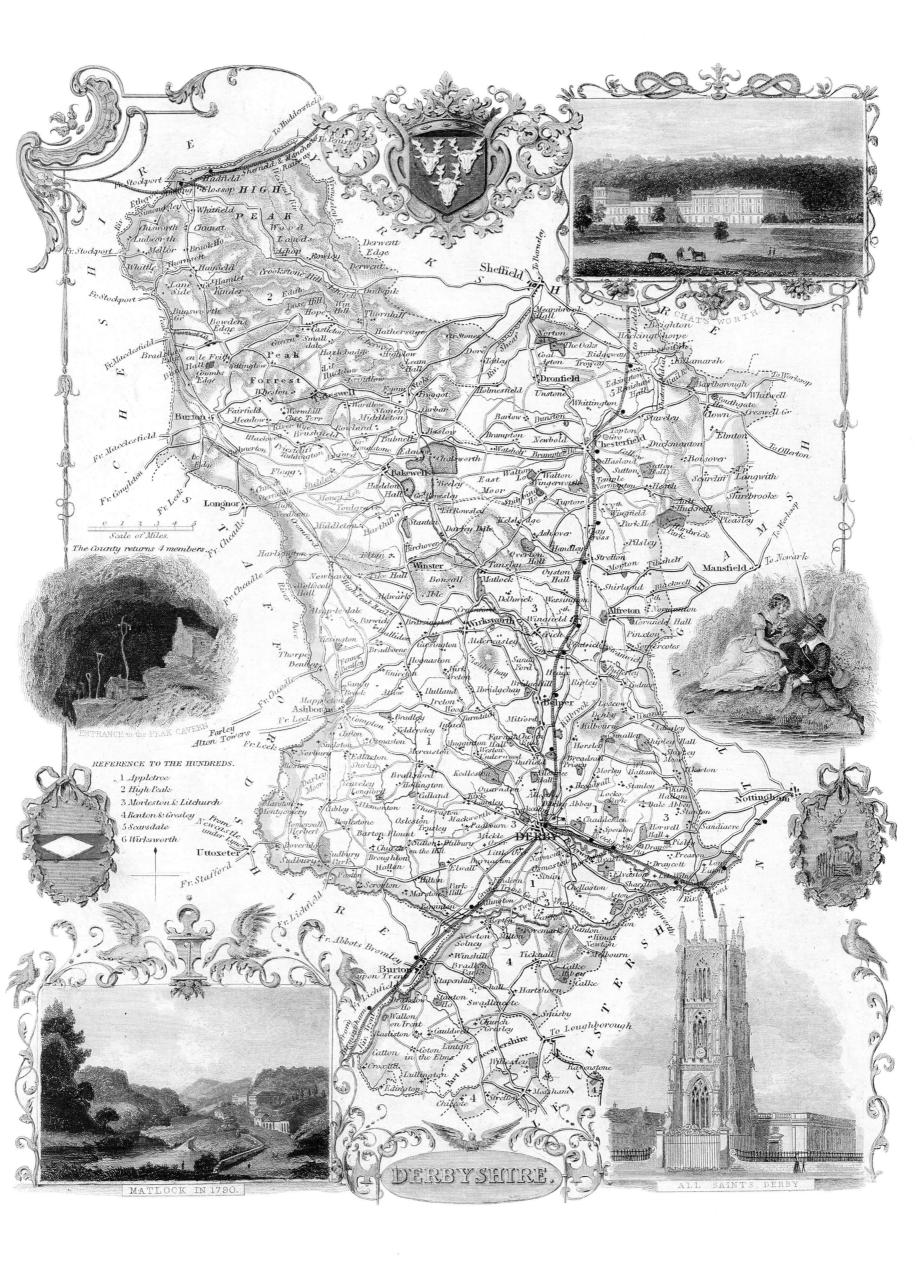

CHATSWORTH.

ENTRANCE to the PEAK CAVERN.

REFERENCE TO THE HUNDREDS.
1 Appletree
2 High Peak
3 Morleston & Litchurch
4 Renton & Gresley
5 Scarsdale
6 Wirksworth

Scale of Miles.
The County returns 4 members.

MATLOCK IN 1790.

DERBYSHIRE.

ALL SAINTS, DERBY.

Devonshire

A county of England, reaching from the Bristol to the English Channel, and bounded by Cornwall, and Somersetshire, and Dorsetshire. It is 69 miles in length, and 60 in breadth, and is divided into 31 hundreds. It is very hilly, and abounds in huge granite rocks, some of whose peaks are above 1500 feet in height. The highland is covered with wide moors, of which Dartmoor is the most extensive. But in the valleys and lower ground the soil is fertile. Its rivers are the Exe, the Culm, the Dart, the Tamar, the Otter, &c. Some parts of its coasts are composed of lofty cliffs, but at others there is a beautiful sandy shore. The air and climate are so mild and salubrious that invalids often retire to its sea-ports for the winter. Limestone, granite, some building-stone, and a species of wood-coal are found here, as well as some kinds of variegated marble. It produces corn, &c. and fruit trees, especially apples, whence much cider is made. Its fisheries also are of value. Exeter is its chief city. Population, 533, 460. It sends 22 members to parliament.

EXETER

The Isca of Ptolemy and Antoninus in Devonshire. The environs of the city are hilly, and afford a variety of delightful prospects. Its port is properly at Topsham, 5 miles below, but vessels of 150 tons come up to the quay here. Here is a noble cathedral, (for it is one of the sees of the bishops of the Church of England), court-houses, public institutions for charity and education, &c. It is the seat of an extensive foreign and domestic commerce, and particularly it had a share in the fisheries of Newfoundland and Greenland. Here are flourishing manufactories of serges and other woollen goods. It is seated on the river Exe, over which it has a long stone bridge. It is 173 miles from London. Markets, Wednesday and Friday. Population, 31,312.

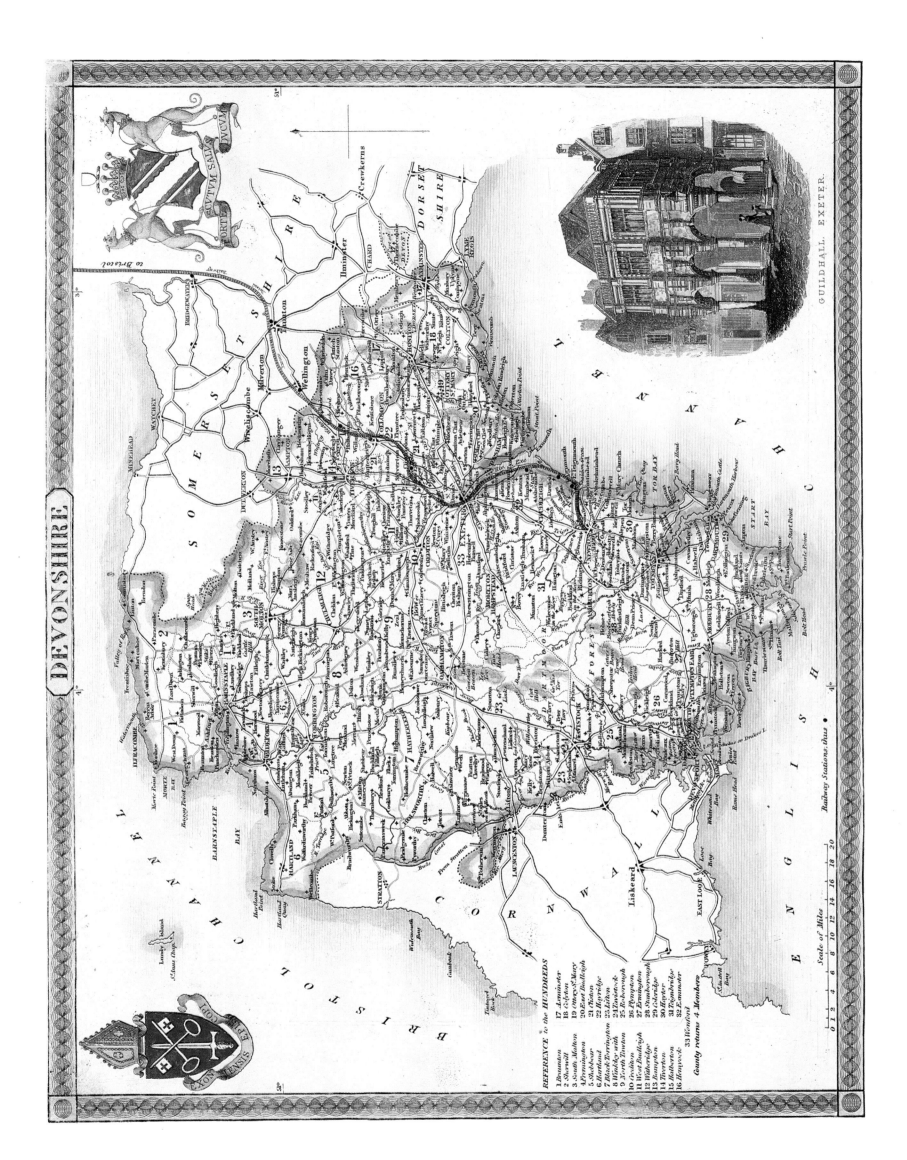

DEVONSHIRE

GUILDHALL, EXETER.

Plymouth and Devonport

Plymouth is a large sea-port, seated between the mouths of the rivers Plym and Tamar, and one of the chief naval magazines in the kingdom, owing to its excellent port or harbour, which capable of safely containing 1000 sail. There are, properly speaking, however, three harbours, Catwater, Sutton Pool, and Hamoaze. The first is the mouth of the Plym, and affords a safe and commodious harbour for merchant ships, but is seldom entered by ships of war. The second is frequented by merchant ships only, and is almost surrounded by the houses of the town. The third inlet, which is the mouth of the Tamar, is the harbour for the reception of the British navy. It is defended by a fort on St. Nicholas Island, and other forts, and particularly by a citadel, called the Haw, which overlooks the town, and is a good land-mark for mariners. A floating bridge plies across the Hamoaze. What is called The Dock, is a separate town, situated about two miles up the Hamoaze, and is now nearly as large as Plymouth itself. Here are some spacious docks, solidly built. It has a good herring fishery, and a considerable trade beside its manufactures, which are of all kinds of goods required in shipping; and the great business arising from the dockyard. It is 210 miles from London. Markets, Monday, Tuesday, and Saturday. Population, 37,058.

Devonport stands at the mouth of the Tamar, and is well fortified. Here is a noble dockyard, and arsenal for the navy. It is a handsome town, and one of growing consequence. Its old name was Plymouth Dock. It is 210 miles from London. Markets, Tuesday, Thursday, and Saturday. Population, 33,820.

ENVIRONS OF PLYMOUTH & DEVONPORT

PLYMOUTH

LIFTON HUNDRED

ROBOROUGH HUNDRED

TAVISTOCK HUNDRED

EAST HUNDRED

WEST HUNDRED

PLYMPTON HUNDRED

ERMINGTON HUNDRED

PLYMOUTH

DEVONPORT

SALTASH

MILLBROOK

PLYMPTON EARLE

Hingston Down

River Tamer

River Tavy

River Tavy

River Lynher

PLYMOUTH SOUND

CAWSAND BAY

BIGBURY BAY

Erm Mouth

Yealm Mouth

Rame Head

Penlee Pt.

Stoke Pt.

Stadden Point

St. Nicholas Island

Scale of Miles.

Dorsetshire

A county of England, lying on the English Channel, bounded by Devonshire, Somersetshire, Wiltshire, and Hampshire. It is about 52 miles in length, and 36 in breadth, and contains 248 parishes. The range of hills belonging to the chalk formation crosses the county, some of which are above 500 feet in height. It is watered by the Stour, the Frome, the Ivel, &c. Some part of the coast is precipitous, and there are some good harbours. Portland Point is at low water connected with the main-land by a long narrow spit of sand. Very good building-stone is obtained here. The greater part of the county is laid down in pasture, the chalk downs affording excellent sheep-walks. The fisheries are also valuable. It has both linen and woollen manufactures. Dorchester is its county town. Population, 175,043. It returns 14 members to parliament.

DORCHESTER

It is a town of great antiquity, and stands by the river Frome. The houses are well built, and it has three handsome streets. It is a corporate and assize town. It has but little trade. It is 120 miles from London. Markets, Wednesday and Saturday. Population, 3249.

PORTLAND

A peninsula near Weymouth, nearly 7 miles round, and exceedingly strong both by nature and art. It is surrounded by inaccessible rocks, except at the landing-place, where there is a strong castle. The whole peninsula is one continuous mass of oolitic rock. The town is small. But the liberty includes several small hamlets. It is 132 miles from London. Population, 2852.

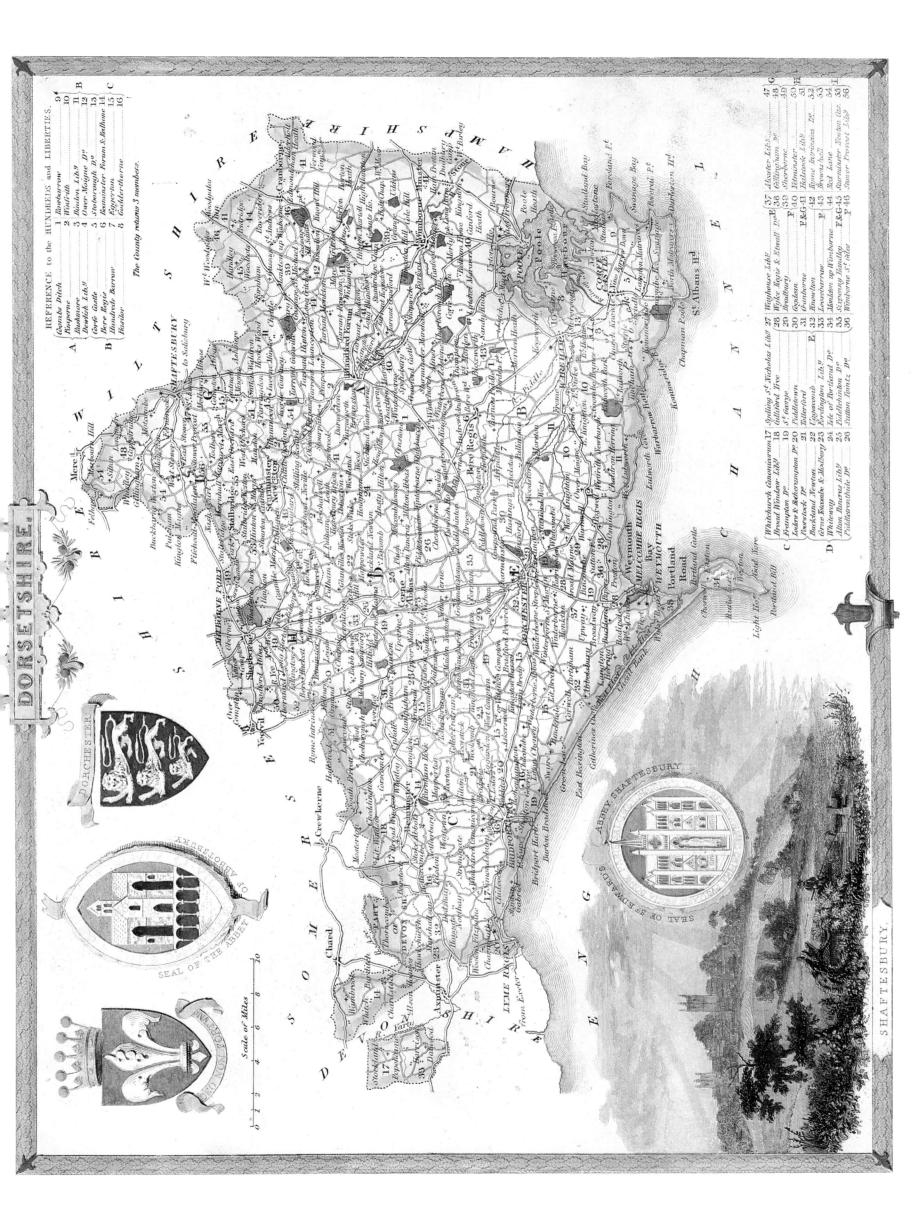

DORSETSHIRE.

REFERENCE to the HUNDREDS and LIBERTIES.

A
1 Rowbarrow
2 Pimperne
3 Badbury
4 Bewlith Lib.y
5 Staborough D.o
6 Ixaminster Forum & Redhone
7 Eggerton
8 Godderthorne

9
10
11 B
12
13
14
15 C
16

The County returns 3 members.

C
17 Whitchurch Canonicorum
18 Broad Windsor Lib.y
19 Frampton P.o
20 Loders & Retterampton P.o
21 Powerstock D.o
22 Buckland Newton.
23 true Barondre & Modbury
24 Whiteway
25 Alton Pancras Lib.y
26 Piddletrenthide D.o

27 Weyhouse Lib.y
28 Wyke Regis & Elwell P.o
29 Radipole
30 Ogsden
31 Cranborne
32 Uppwould
33 Ferdington Lib.y
34 Hanston up Winborne
35 Sixpenny Handley
36 Winborne St. Giles

37 Alcester Lib.s
38 Gillingham D.o
39 Sherborne
40 Wimecaster
41 Halsrock Lib.s
42 Rome Intrinsica D.o
43 Browns hill
44 Red Lane
45 Starminster Newton Gao.
46 Winborne Provost Lib.t

SEAL OF THE ABBEY

DORCHESTER

SEAL OF ST EDWARDS. ABBEY SHAFTESBURY.

Scale of Miles

SHAFTESBURY.

Durham

A county of England, lying on the German Ocean, and bounded by Northumberland, Cumberland, Westmoreland, and Yorkshire. It is about 40 miles in length and 30 in breadth, and contains 1 city, 8 market towns, and 113 parishes. It is hilly, and some points are nearly 2000 feet high. There are wide moors amongst the hills, and other tracts completely uncultivated. There are some islands on the coast, Holy Island being the largest. The coast is cliffy in some parts; other parts are shelving sands. The principal rivers are the Wear, the Tees, the Tyne, and the Derwent. Coal, iron, lead, mill-stone grit, lime-stone, &c., are found here abundantly. The east and south parts of the county are fruitful in corn and pasture, and have a milder air than the other parts. It sends to other parts of the United Kingdom, and to foreign countries, both its native productions, and the goods it manufactures, such as coarse woollen goods, sail-cloth, steel, glass, iron, &c. &c. This county was formerly under the special jurisdiction of the bishop of Durham as a Prince Palatine, but in 1836 the palatinate was vested in the crown. Population, 342,284. It returns 10 members to parliament.

DURHAM

The capital of the county, is an ancient city, situated on seven hills, and surrounded by others more lofty, in a beautiful winding of the river Wear, along the banks of which are pleasant walks, covered with woods, and edged with lofty crags. Here are woollen manufactories, and iron-works. The cathedral is a fine building, and the castle is a curious relic of antiquity. A university was established here by Oliver Cromwell, which, under the control of the Church of England, is now a flourishing institution for arts and learning. It is a bishop's see. It is 257 miles from London. Market, Saturday. Population, 14,151.

HOLY-ISLAND

A small island on the coast of Northumberland, one mile and a half from the nearest land. It is two miles and a quarter long, and one in breadth, and consists of one continued plain. The soil is rocky; and it has but one small town, or village, standing on a rising ground, consisting of a few scattered houses, chiefly inhabited by fishermen, with a church. Under the castle, which stands at the southern point, on almost a perpendicular rock, near 60 feet high, and is accessible only by a narrow and winding pass, cut out of the rock, on its southern side, there is a commodious bay, or harbour, defended by a blockhouse. It has plenty of fish and fowl; the west part is left wholly to the rabbits; and there is not a tree on the island. The monastery, which covered near four acres, is entirely in ruins. It is a peninsula at ebb-tide. It is 340 miles from London. Population 809.

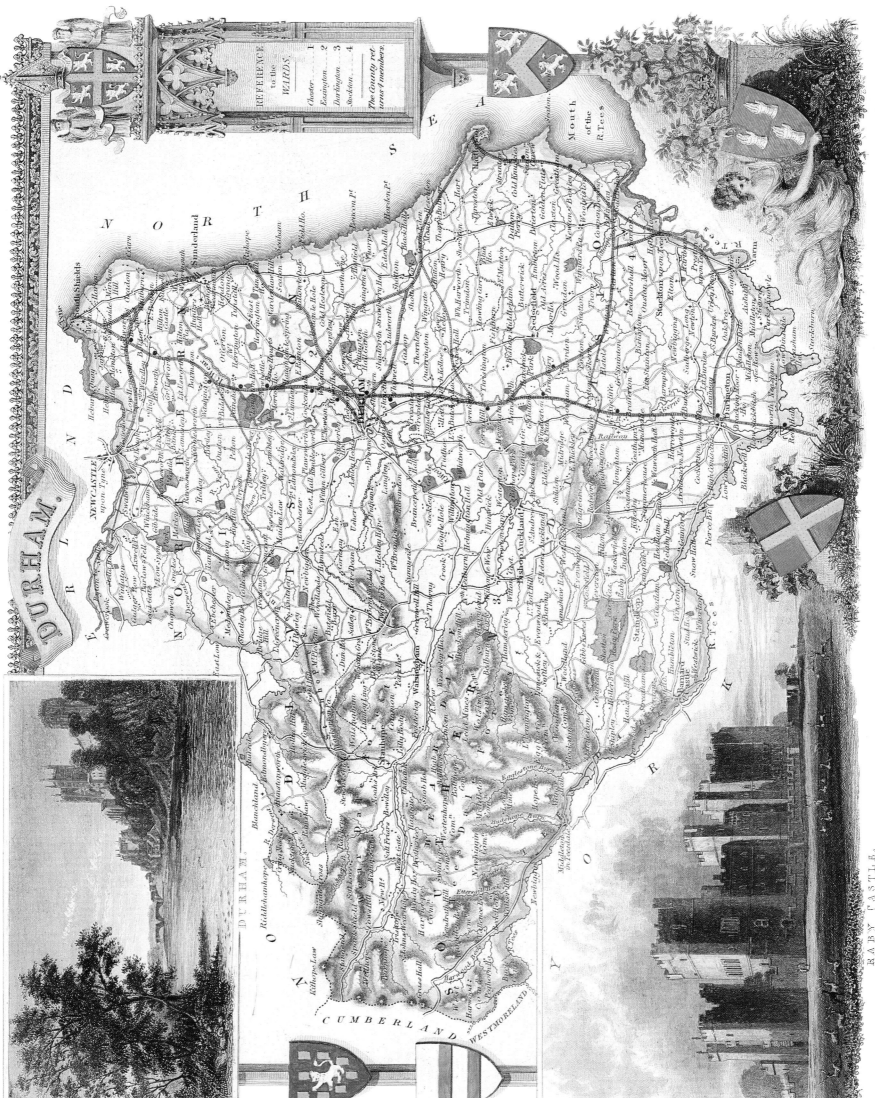

DURHAM.

NORTH SEA

Mouth of the R. Tees

R. Tees

NORTHUMBERLAND

NEWCASTLE upon Tyne

CHESTER WARD

DARLINGTON WARD

STOCKTON WARD

EASINGTON WARD

CUMBERLAND

WESTMORELAND

YORK

DURHAM

RABY CASTLE.

Essex

A county in the east of England, lying on the German Ocean, bounded by Suffolk, Cambridge, Hertfordshire, and Middlesex; and separated by the Thames from Kent. It is about 54 miles long, and 48 broad, and is divided into 18 hundreds. Its surface is level, yet sufficiently varied not to be monotonous; but, excepting at a few points, the coast is flat and marshy. The rivers are the Thames, the Stour, the Lea, the Chelmer, the Blackwater, the Coln, &c. The soil is varied, but on the whole it is an admirable corn county. It has also excellent pastures; and some woods of considerable extent, such as Epping Forest. It produces in addition to farm-produce, oysters called natives, and some few textile manufactures. Chelmsford is its county town. Colchester is a place of some importance.

COLCHESTER

It is situated on a fine eminence near the Coln, which is navigable within three miles of the town for ships of large burden, and for hoys and small barks to a place called the Hythe, where is a quay close to the houses. Here is a manufactory of baize and says; and it is noted for oysters called natives. It has an ancient castle, and some other fine buildings both ancient and modern. It is a principal station on the Eastern Counties Railway. It is 51 miles from London. Markets, Wednesday and Saturday. Population, 17,790.

CHELMSFORD

It is pleasantly situated in a valley, at the confluence of the Chelmer and the Cam, the gardens of the inhabitants on each side of the town extending to those rivers. Here are some good public buildings, and a fountain, or conduit, of excellent water; and the assizes and quarter sessions for the county are held here. The great eastern road from London formerly passed through it, and the railroad now going by it at a short distance, has nearly doubled the size of the town. It is 29 miles from London. Market for corn, cattle, and provisions, Friday. Population, 6789.

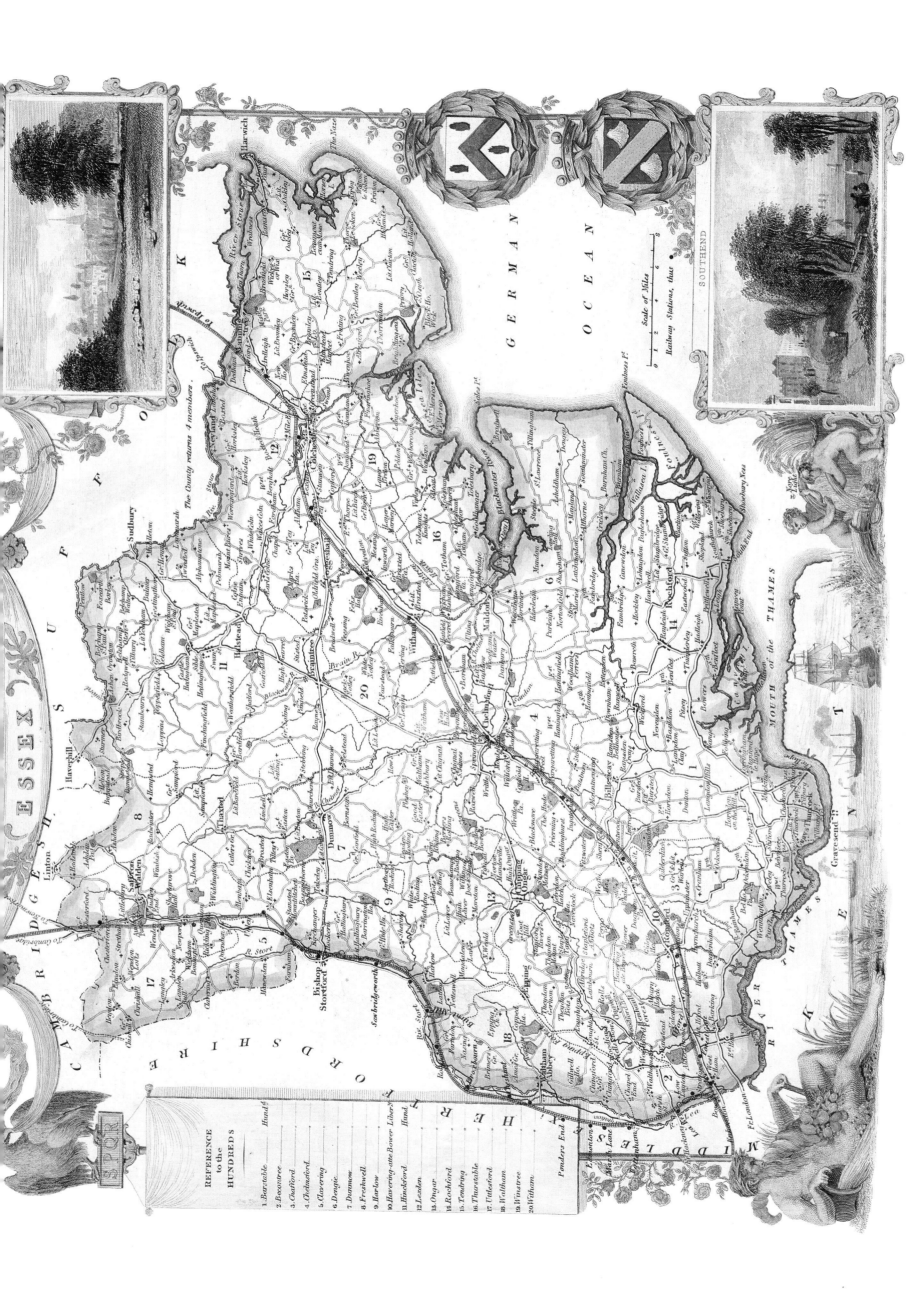

ESSEX

SOUTHEND

GERMAN OCEAN

MOUTH OF THE THAMES

RIVER THAMES

SUFFOLK

CAMBRIDGESHIRE

HERTFORDSHIRE

MIDDLESEX

KENT

Scale of Miles

Railway Stations, thus

The County returns 4 members.

Harwich

Colchester

Chelmsford

Maldon

Sudbury

Saffron Walden

Bishop Stortford

Epping

Ongar

Rochford

Gloucestershire

A county of England, bounded by Monmouthshire, Herefordshire, Worcestershire, Warwickshire, Oxfordshire, Wiltshire, and Somersetshire. It extends in length more than 60 miles, but is not more than 26 in breadth. It is divided into 13 hundreds, which contain one city, 27 market towns, 280 parishes, and 1229 villages. The soil and appearance of this county vary in different parts, but the air is healthy throughout; sharp on the east or hilly part, which contains the Cotswold Hills, but mild in the rich vale of Severn, which occupies the centre. The west part, which is the smallest district, is varied by hill and dale, and chiefly occupied by the Forest of Dean, which was once full of oak trees, but now occupied by coal-mines and iron-works. The staple commodities are cheese, cider, perry, bacon, grain, and fish, besides its manufactories of woollen cloths, hats, leather, paper, bar-iron, edge tools, nails, brass, &c. Its rivers are the Severn, the Warwickshire Avon, the Lower Avon, the Wye, Thames, Coln, Lech, Windrush, Evenlode, Churn, Leden, Swiliate, Caron, and Stour. Gloucester is its chief place. Population 431,383. It sends 15 members to parliament.

GLOUCESTER

The chief city, containing 5 parish churches, besides its ancient and magnificent cathedral. It is well built, and its four principal streets are greatly admired for the regularity of their junction in the centre of the town; besides which there are several smaller ones, all well paved. Here is a good stone bridge over the Severn, the lowest down that river, with a quay, wharf, and custom-house. The manufacture of pins, &c., is not so flourishing. It is seated on the east side of the Severn, where, by its two streams, it forms the Isle of Alney. It is 106 miles from London. Market, Wednesday. Fairs on April 5, July 5, September 28, and November 28, the latter chiefly for fat hogs. Population, 14,152.

CHELTENHAM

It is noted for its mineral waters, and extensive prospects from its adjoining hills. It is much improved of late years, with a new market-house, and many handsome public buildings. It used to have a little trade from the neighbouring manufacturing towns; but now derives all its subsistence from its spa. It is 95 miles from London. Market, Thursday. Population, 31,411.

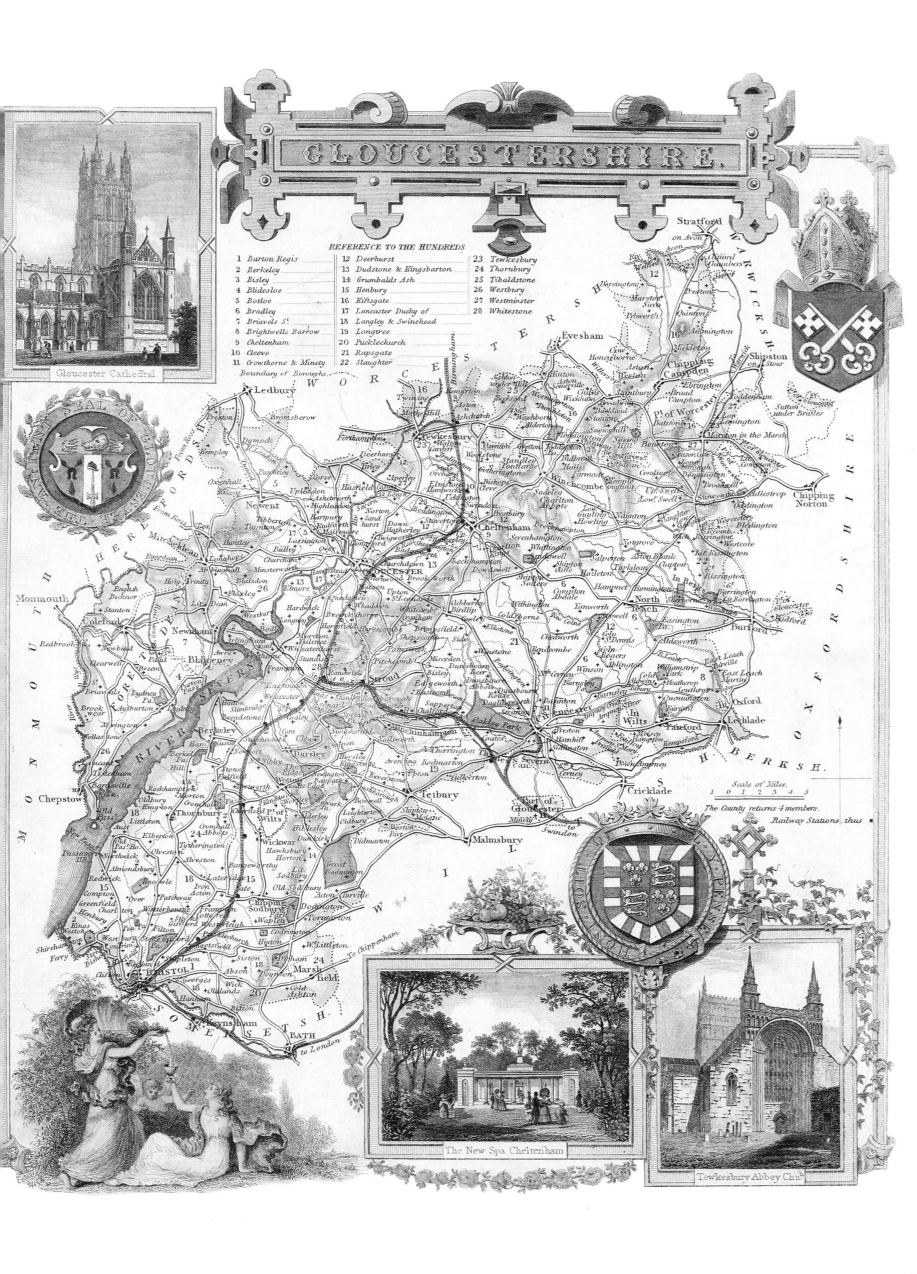

GLOUCESTERSHIRE.

Gloucester Cathedral.

REFERENCE TO THE HUNDREDS

1 Barton Regis	12 Deerhurst	23 Tewkesbury
2 Berkeley	13 Dudstone & Kingsbarton	24 Thornbury
3 Bisley	14 Grumbalds Ash	25 Tibaldstone
4 Blidesloe	15 Henbury	26 Westbury
5 Botloe	16 Kiftsgate	27 Westminster
6 Bradley	17 Lancaster Duchy of	28 Whitestone
7 Briavels St.	18 Langley & Swinehead	
8 Brightwells Barrow	19 Longtree	
9 Cheltenham	20 Pucklechurch	
10 Cleeve	21 Rapsgate	
11 Growthorne & Minety	22 Slaughter	
	Boundary of Boroughs.	

Scale of Miles.

The County returns 4 members.

Railway Stations, thus

The New Spa Cheltenham

Tewkesbury Abbey Chu.

Hampshire

A county of England, lying on the English Channel, bounded by Dorsetshire, Wiltshire, Berkshire, Surrey, and Sussex. It extends, exclusively of the Isle of Wight, 42 miles in length, and 38 in breadth. It is divided into 39 hundreds, which contain 1 city, 20 market towns, 253 parishes, and 1062 villages. It is one of the most fertile counties in England. The range of chalk downs runs through the north part of the county. Its products are the finest corn and hops, very large flocks of cattle and sheep, with excellent wool, bacon, honey, and timber. For the last it has been particularly famous, on account of its great woods, of which the principal are the New Forest, and the Forest of East Bere. The principal rivers are the Avon, the Test or Tese, the Itchen, and the Stour. The Isle of Wight is included in its boundaries. Opposite to the island are Portsmouth and Southampton harbours. It has good fisheries, and some small manufactories. Winchester is the county town. Population 355,004. It returns 19 members to parliament.

Winchester

It stands on the Itchin, and has six parish churches, besides the cathedral, which is a large and beautiful structure, and in which are interred several Saxon kings and queens. The other remarkable buildings are the bishop's palace, the hall where the assizes are kept, and the college or school, which last is without walls. It is 62 miles from London. Markets, Wednesday and Saturday. Population, 10,732.

Southampton

It is pleasantly situated on a fine inlet of the sea, called Trissanton Bay, or Southampton Water, which is navigable almost to the head for vessels of considerable burden; and the two principal rivers that flow into it (the Itchen and the Test or Tese) admit small crafts some way up the country. The town is situated between these two rivers. It is a handsome place, with some fine public buildings, and a considerable trade. Ship-building, and the manufacture of sails, cordage, &c. are also carried on. It is a place of some resort for sea-bathing. It is 75 miles from London. Markets, Tuesday, Thursday, and Saturday. Population, 27,744.

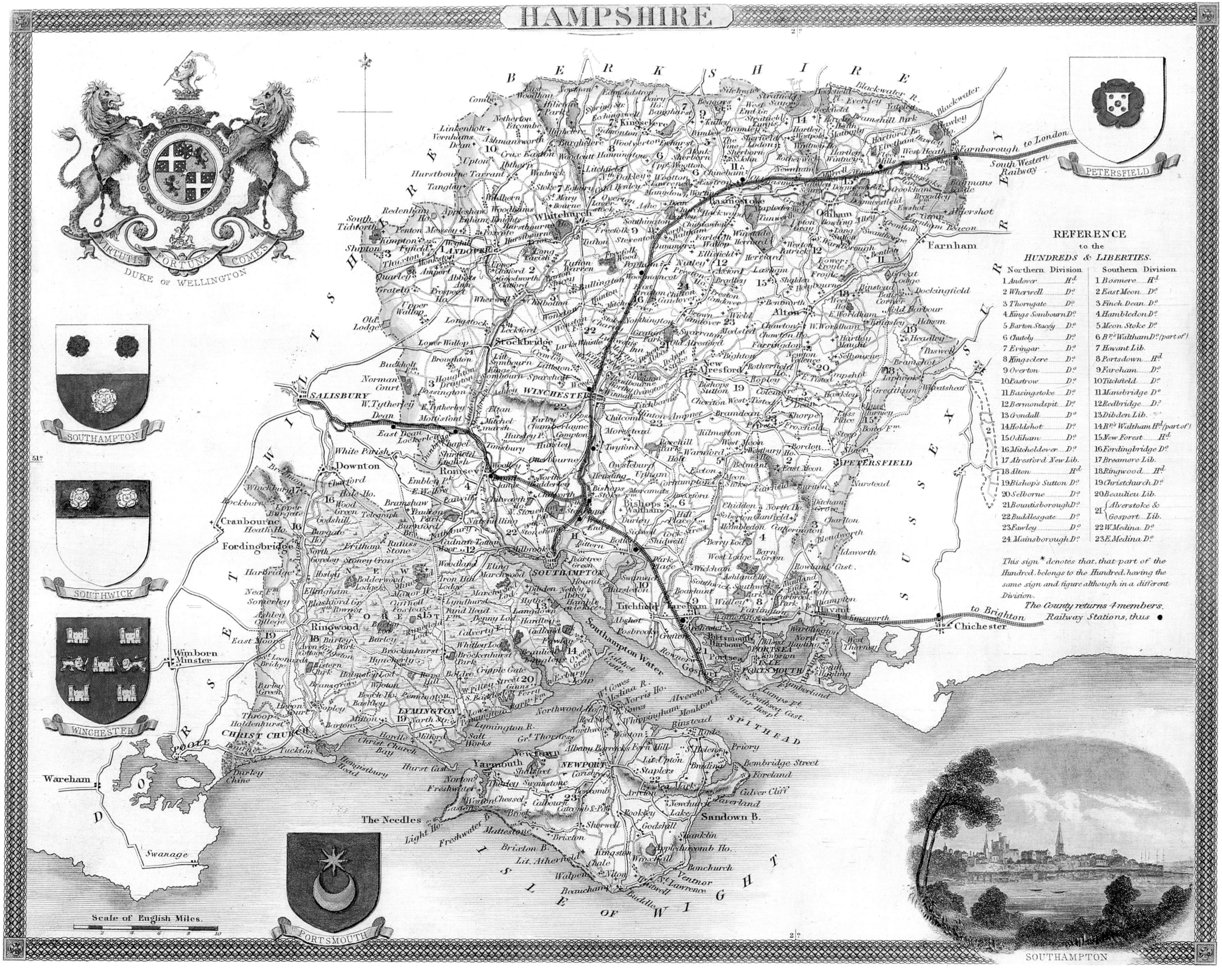
HAMPSHIRE
VIRTUTIS FORTUNA COMES
DUKE OF WELLINGTON
SOUTHAMPTON
SOUTHWICK
WINCHESTER
PORTSMOUTH
PETERSFIELD
BERKSHIRE
WILTSHIRE
SURREY
SUSSEX
DORSET
ISLE OF WIGHT
SPITHEAD
Southampton Water
SALISBURY
WINCHESTER
SOUTHAMPTON
PORTSMOUTH
LYMINGTON
CHRIST CHURCH
NEWPORT
Farnborough to London
South Western Railway
to Brighton
Chichester
Farnham
Wareham
Wimborn Minster
Swanage
POOLE
The Needles
REFERENCE
to the
HUNDREDS & LIBERTIES.
Northern Division
1 Andover Hd.
2 Wherwell Do.
3 Thorngate Do.
4 Kings Sombourn Do.
5 Barton Stacey Do.
6 Chutely Do.
7 Evingar Do.
8 Kingsclere Do.
9 Overton Do.
10 Pastrow Do.
11 Basingstoke Do.
12 Bermondspit Do.
13 Crondall Do.
14 Holdshot Do.
15 Odiham Do.
16 Mitcheldever Do.
17 Alresford New Lib.
18 Alton Hd.
19 Bishop's Sutton Do.
20 Selborne Do.
21 Bountisborough Do.
22 Buddlesgate Do.
23 Fawley Do.
24 Mainsborough Do.
Southern Division
1 Bosmere Hd.
2 East Meon Do.
3 Finch Dean Do.
4 Hambledon Do.
5 Meon Stoke Do.
6 Bps. Waltham Do. (part of)
7 Havant Lib.
8 Portsdown Hd.
9 Fareham Do.
10 Titchfield Do.
11 Mansbridge Do.
12 Redbridge Do.
13 Dibden Lib.
14 Bps. Waltham Hd. (part of)
15 New Forest Hd.
16 Fordingbridge Do.
17 Breamore Lib.
18 Ringwood Hd.
19 Christchurch Do.
20 Beaulieu Lib.
21 Alverstoke & Gosport Lib.
22 W. Medina Do.
23 E. Medina Do.
This sign * denotes that, that part of the Hundred, belongs to the Hundred, having the same sign and figure although in a different Division.
The County returns 4 members.
Railway Stations, thus ●
Scale of English Miles.
SOUTHAMPTON

Portsmouth

It is situated on the island of Portsea, and is very strongly fortified. The royal docks and yards resemble distinct towns, under a government separate from the garrison. Here is also a fine arsenal for laying up the cannon. The harbour is one of the finest in the world, as there is water sufficient for the largest ships; and it is so very capacious, that the whole English navy could ride here in safety. Across the harbour's mouth, a floating steam-bridge plies continually between this town and Gosport. Opposite the town is the spacious road of Spithead. The town is extensive, and has some fine streets and public walks. The churches and chapels are fine buildings. It is 72 miles from London. Markets, Tuesday, Thursday, and Saturday. Population, 9354, and of Portsea, 43,678.

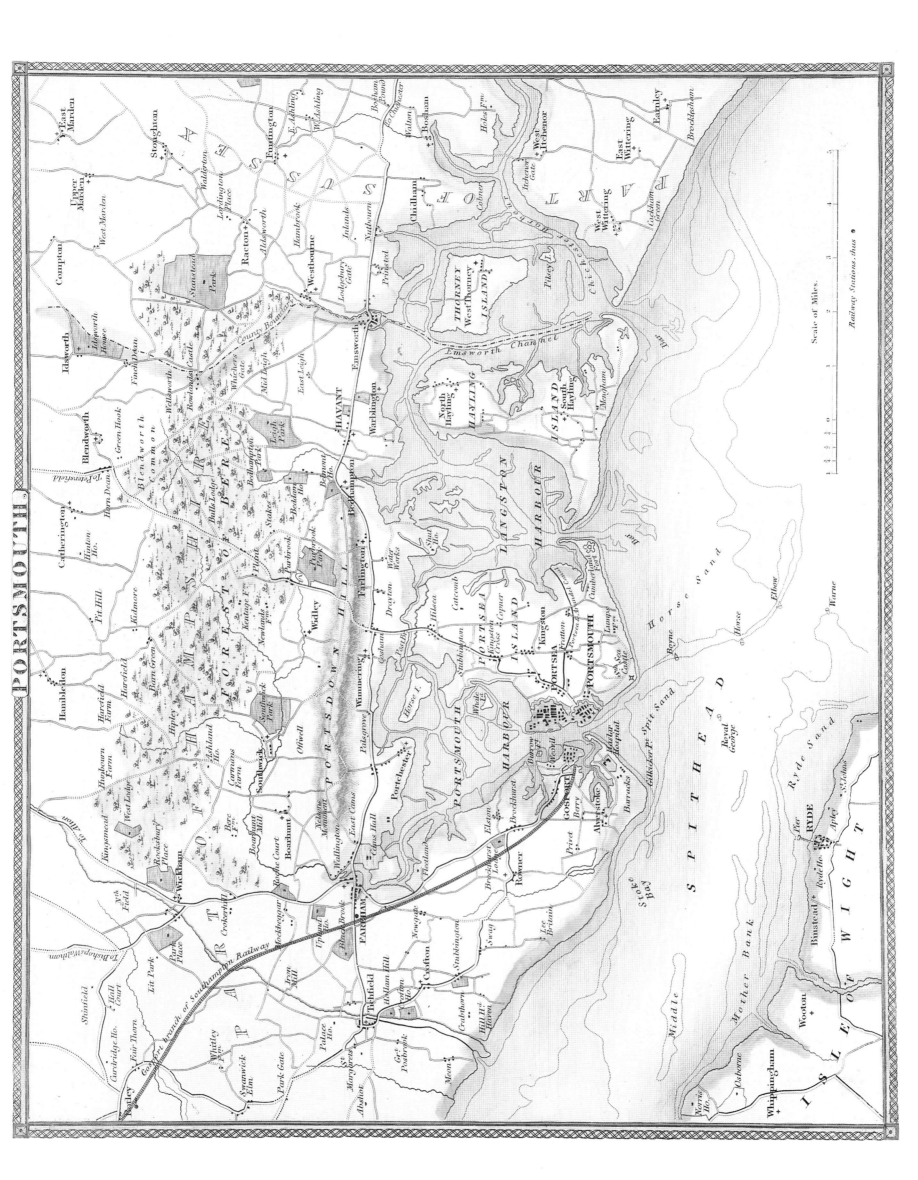

PORTSMOUTH.

Scale of Miles.

Railway Stations, thus ⊙

Herefordshire

A county of England lying next to Wales, and bounded by Shropshire, Gloucestershire, Worcestershire, and Monmouthshire. It extends about 38 miles from north to south, and 33 from east to west. It is divided into 11 hundreds, which contain 1 city, 6 market towns, 176 parishes, and 391 villages. The air is healthy, the climate mild, the soil generally fertile, producing wheat, barley, oats, clover, turnips, &c., a principal part of the land being employed in tillage; the face of the country is rich, beautiful, and picturesque; and it abounds with wood. It produces excellent cider; and the pastures abound with sheep, whose wool is of very fine quality. The principal rivers are the Wye, Munnow, Lug, and Frome, all of which are well stored with fish and salmon in particular. Hereford is its chief place. Population, 113,878. It sends seven members to parliament.

HEREFORD

It is pleasantly and commodiously seated among delightful meadows and rich corn-fields, and is almost encompassed by the Wye and two other rivers, over which are two bridges. It is a large place, and had six parish churches, but two of them were demolished in the civil wars. It had also a castle, which has been long destroyed. It is a bishop's see, and the cathedral is a handsome structure. The chief manufacture is gloves, many of which are sent to London. The streets are broad and paved. It is 136 miles from London. Markets, Wednesday, Friday, and Saturday. Population, 10,921.

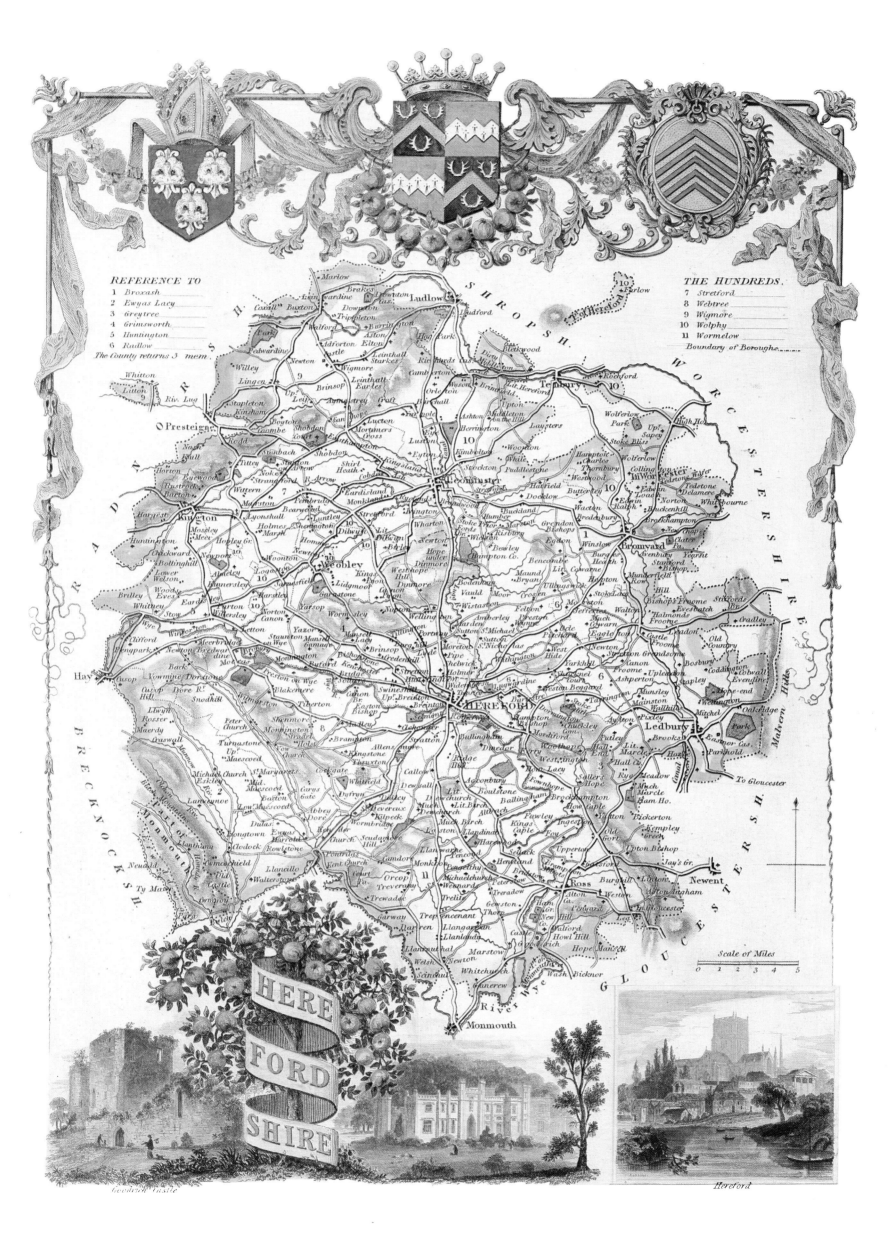

REFERENCE TO
1 Broxash
2 Ewyas Lacy
3 Greytree
4 Grimsworth
5 Huntington
6 Radlow
The County returns 3 mem.

THE HUNDREDS.
7 Stretford
8 Webtree
9 Wigmore
10 Wolphy
11 Wormelow
Boundary of Borough

SHROPSH.

WORCESTERSHIRE

RADNORSH.

BRECKNOCKSH.

Monmouth

GLOUCESTERSH.

River Wye

Scale of Miles
0 1 2 3 4 5

HERE FORD SHIRE

Goodrich Castle

Hereford

Hertfordshire

A county of England, bounded by Middlesex, Essex, Cambridgeshire, Bedfordshire, and Buckinghamshire. It is about 35 miles long, and 25 broad. It is divided into 8 hundreds, and contains 2 boroughs and 12 market towns. The chalk hills are the only heights, and they are, in general, not great, though one point is above 900 feet; but they render the surface undulating, and greatly enhance the beauty of the rural scenes it abounds in. The Colne and the Lea are its chief rivers. The New River, which supplies good part of London with Water, begins near Ware. It is yet well wooded; but agriculture prospers, and corn, cattle, sheep, &c. &c. are plentifully produced. There are also many gardens cultivated for the supply of the London market. Hertford is its chief place. Population, 157,207. It sends 7 members to parliament.

HERTFORD

It is seated on the Lea, and is a neat place. The remains of an old castle have been converted into a high school in connexion with the East India college. The chief buildings are those belonging to the county. It is a great place for malting. It is 26 miles from London. Market, Saturday. Population, 5450.

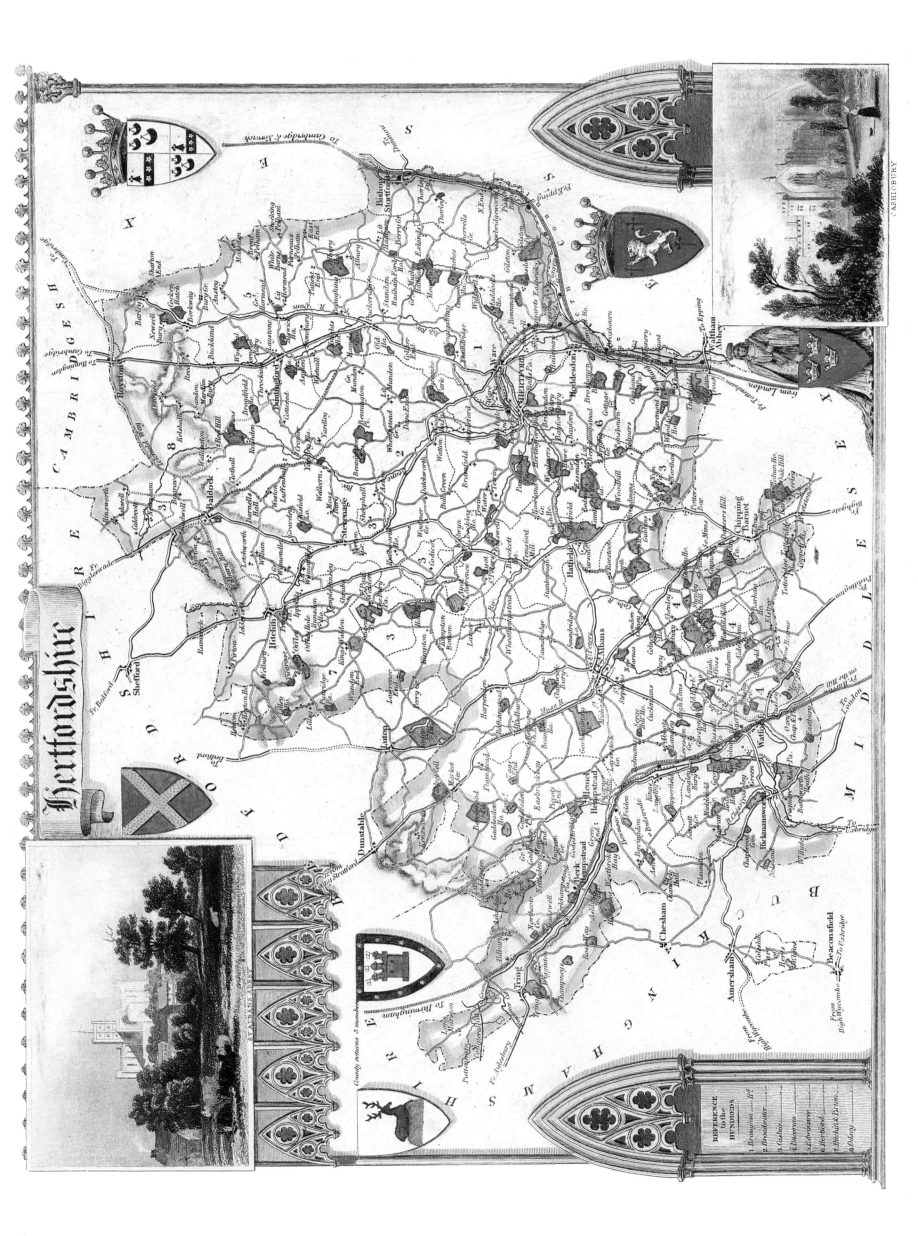

Hertfordshire

CASHIOBURY

ST ALBANS ABBEY

REFERENCE to the HUNDREDS

1. Braughin Ht
2. Broadwater
3. Cashio
4. Dacorum
5. Edwinstree
6. Hertford
7. Hitchin & Pirton
8. Odsey

Huntingdonshire

A county of England, bounded by Northamptonshire, Cambridgeshire, and Bedfordshire. It is 22 miles long, and about 18 broad. The principal rivers are the Ouse and Nen. It is divided into 4 hundreds, which contain 5 market towns, 78 parishes, and 279 villages. The borders of the Ouse, which flows across the south east part, consist of fertile and very beautiful meadows. The middle and western parts are finely varied in their surface, fertile in corn, and sprinkled with woods. The whole upland part was, in ancient times, a forest, peculiarly adapted for hunting, whence the name of the county took its rise. The north east part consists of fens, which join those of Ely; but they are drained, so as to afford rich pasturage for cattle, and even large crops of corn; and in the midst of them are shallow pools, abounding with fish. The largest of these is a lake of considerable size, called Whittlesea Mere. Its chief commodities are corn, malt, and cheese; and they fatten abundance of cattle. Huntingdon is its chief town. Population, 58,549. It sends 4 members to parliament.

Huntingdon

Called by the Saxons Hunter's Down. It has 2 churches, a handsome market-place, and a good grammar-school. It was once very large, having 15 churches, which, in Camden's time, were reduced to 4, and now to 2; and it is still a populous, trading place. It is seated on the river Ouse, over which it has a handsome stone bridge, leading to Godmanchester. It is 65 miles from London. Markets, Monday and Saturday. Population, 3507.

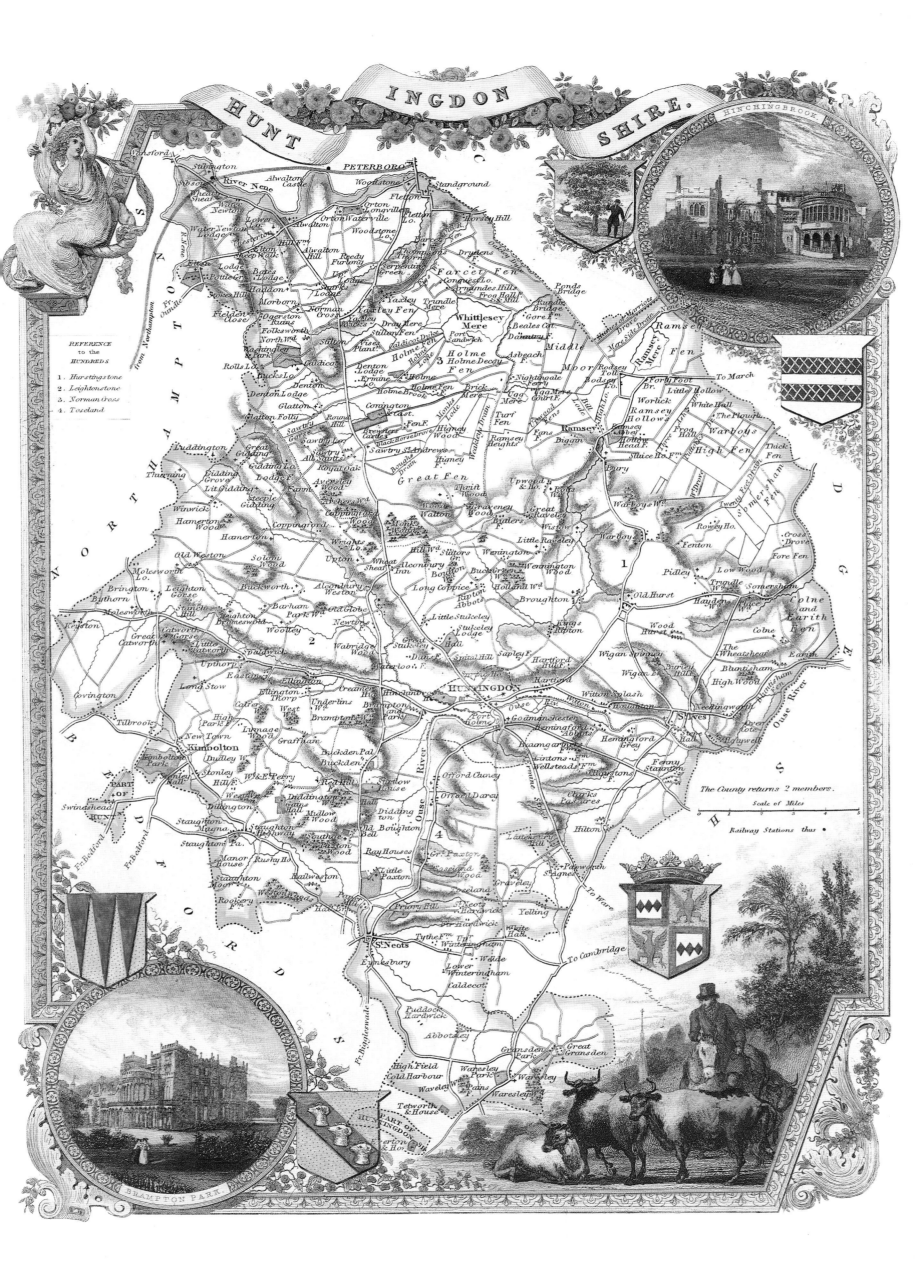

HUNTINGDON SHIRE.

HINCHINGBROOK.

REFERENCE
to the
HUNDREDS

1. *Hurstingstone*
2. *Leightonstone*
3. *Normancross*
4. *Toseland*

The County returns 2 members.

Scale of Miles

Railway Stations thus •

BRAMPTON PARK.

Kent

A county of the south of England, washed by the English Channel, the Straits of Dover, and the German Ocean; and bounded by Surrey, Sussex, Essex, and Middlesex. It is about 58 miles in length, and 35 in breadth. It is divided into five lathes, under each of which are several hundreds, which contain 2 cities, 39 market towns, 408 parish churches, and 1180 villages. In the soil and face of the country there is great diversity. The banks of the Thames are low and marshy, but backed by a range of chalky eminences, sometimes rising to a moderate height, which extend to the sea at Dover, and form those lofty white cliffs, which present so striking an appearance at sea, and probably originated the name of Albion. The south part of Kent, called the Weald, is a flat, woody tract, of a clayey soil; fertile, but not very healthy. It terminates in the great marsh of Romney. The midland and western districts are a happy mixture of hill and vale, arable and pasture, equal in pleasantness, and variety of products, to any part of England. This county produces, besides corn, &c., large quantities of hops; fruits of various kinds, especially cherries and apples, of which there are large orchards for the London markets; madder for dyeing; timber, &c. The downs and the marshes afford excellent pasture for sheep and cattle. Its manufactures are but trifling. The principal rivers, besides the Thames, are the Medway, Darent, Stour, Cray, and Rother. Maidstone is the county town. Population, 548,337. It sends 18 members to parliament.

MAIDSTONE

It is a large place, consisting of four principal streets, which intersect each other. By means of the Medway, over which it has a fine bridge, it enjoys a brisk trade in exporting timber, flour, apples, nuts, and other commodities of the county, particularly hops, of which there are numerous plantations around it, as well as orchards of cherries. Here are likewise some capital paper-mills, and a manufactory of linen thread originally introduced by the Flemings. Here is a large gaol, and very extentive barracks for horse-soldiers. The town-hall, corn-exchange, &c. are good buildings. It is 35 miles from London. Market, Thursday, and another market on the second Tuesday in every month. Population, 18,086.

GREENWICH

It is situated on the Thames, and is now almost one with London. It is notorious as a place of resort for pleasure-seekers from the metropolis. Here is the National Observatory, well furnished with all requisite astronomical instruments; from the meridian of which the English reckon their degrees of longitude. Here, too, is the grand Naval Hospital, in which above 3000 disabled seamen from the fleet are kept at the expense of the nation. Schools, &c. are connected with it. It is 5 miles from London. Population, 29,595.

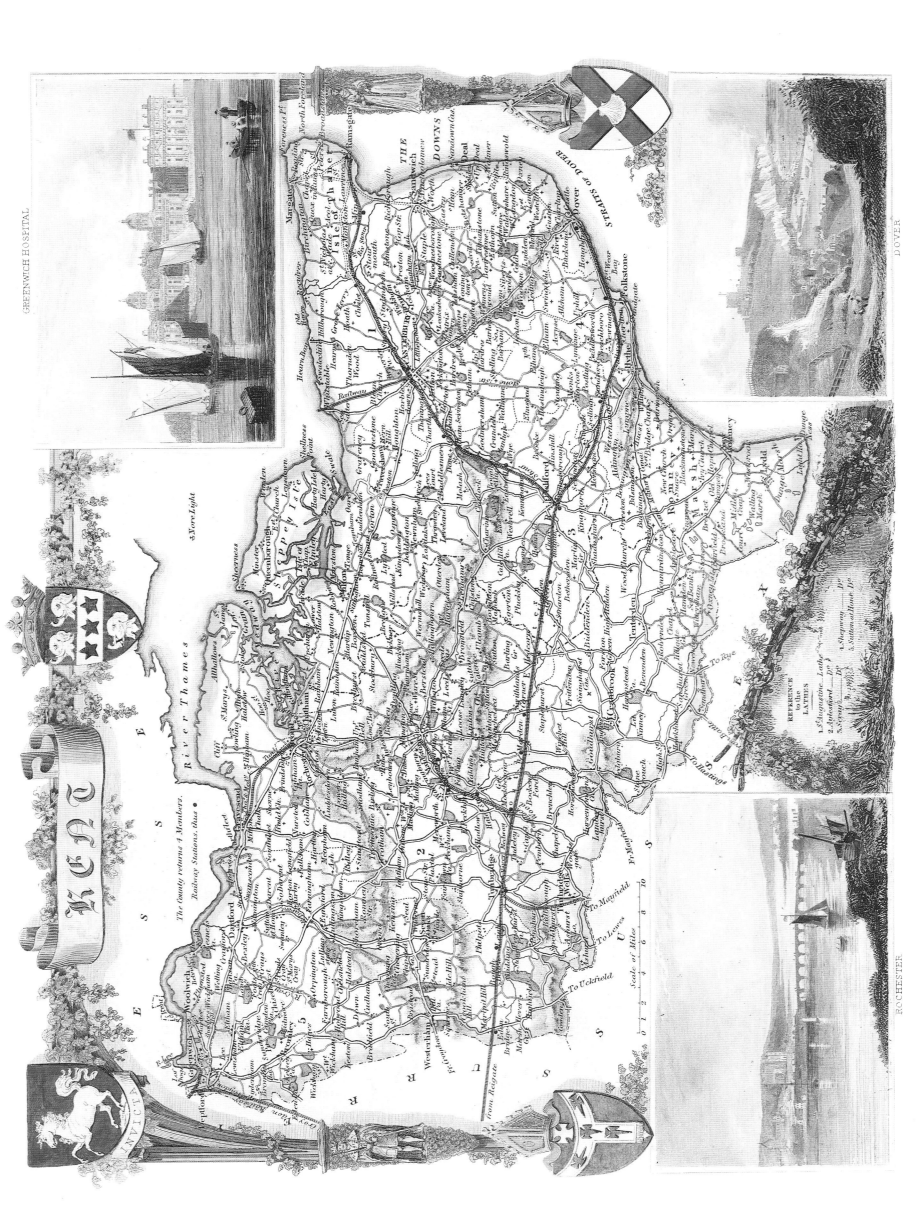

GREENWICH HOSPITAL

DOVER

ROCHESTER

KENT

INVICTA

The County returns 4 Members.
Railway Stations, thus ●

Scale of Miles

REFERENCE
to the
LATHES
1. S.t Augustine ... Lathe of ......
2. Aylesford ...... D.o
3. Scray .... D.o
4. Shepway ...... D.o
5. Sutton at Hone. D.o

Lancashire

A county of England, lying on the Irish Sea, and bounded by Cumberland, Westmoreland, Yorkshire, and Cheshire. It is 75 miles in length, and 30 in breadth. It is divided into 6 hundreds, which contain 27 market towns, 62 parishes, and 894 villages. This county comprises a variety of soil and face of country; there being mountains of more than 2000 feet high, in the north and eastern parts, with wide moorlands or heaths amongst them; extensive bogs or mosses, which yield only turf for fuel, and are very dangerous; and some most fertile land for agricultural purposes. it yields iron, coal, slate, and other building-stones; salt, &c. &c. Grazing is more attended to than agriculture. The fisheries, both in the rivers and the sea, are valuable. As a commercial and manufacturing county, Lancashire is distinguished beyond most others in the kingdom. Its principal manufactures are linen, silk, and cotton goods; fustians, counterpanes, shalloons, baize, serges, tapes, small wares, hats, sail-cloth, sacking, pins, iron goods, cast plate-glass, &c. Of the commerce of this county, it may suffice to observe, that Liverpool is now the second port in the United Kingdom. The principal rivers are the Mersey, Irwell, Ribble, Lune, Leven, Wyre, Hodder, Roche, Duddon, Winster, Ken, and Calder, and it has two considerable lakes, Windermere and Coniston Water. Lancaster is the county town. Population, 1,667,054. It returns 26 members to parliament.

Lancaster

An ancient, well-built, and improving town. On the summit of a hill stands the castle, which is not ancient, but large and strong, and now serves both as the shire house and the county gaol. On the top of this castle is a square tower, called John of Gaunt's Chair, where there is a fine prospect of the mountains of Cumberland, and of the course of the Lune; the view towards the sea extending to the Isle of Man. The town hall is a handsome structure. Lancaster carries on some foreign trade, especially to the West Indies, America, and the Baltic. The exports are hardware, woollen goods, candles, and cabinet work, for the making of which last it is noted; and it has also a manufacture of sail-cloth. It is seated on the river Lune, which here forms a port for vessels of moderate size, and over which it has a new stone bridge of five elliptical arches. It is 235 miles from London. Markets, Wednesday and Saturday, and one on every other Wednesday for cattle. Population, 24,707.

Liverpool

It stands on the Mersey, and by its position, and wealth, has become the second port in the kingdom. It is, on the whole, a very handsome and commodious town; and the public buildings are numerous, and highly ornamental to it. The churches, the municipal edifices, the custom-house, the exchange, the charitable institutions, the markets, and the theatres, seem to have been constructed for the gratification of taste, as well as for their various and peculiar uses. But the docks are the most remarkable feature of the town; and the construction of them has enabled it to take its distinguished position in the commerce of the world. Its inland trade is aided by the rivers Irwell and Weaver, by the canals, and by the railroads, which converge there. It is 206 miles from London. Population, 286,487.

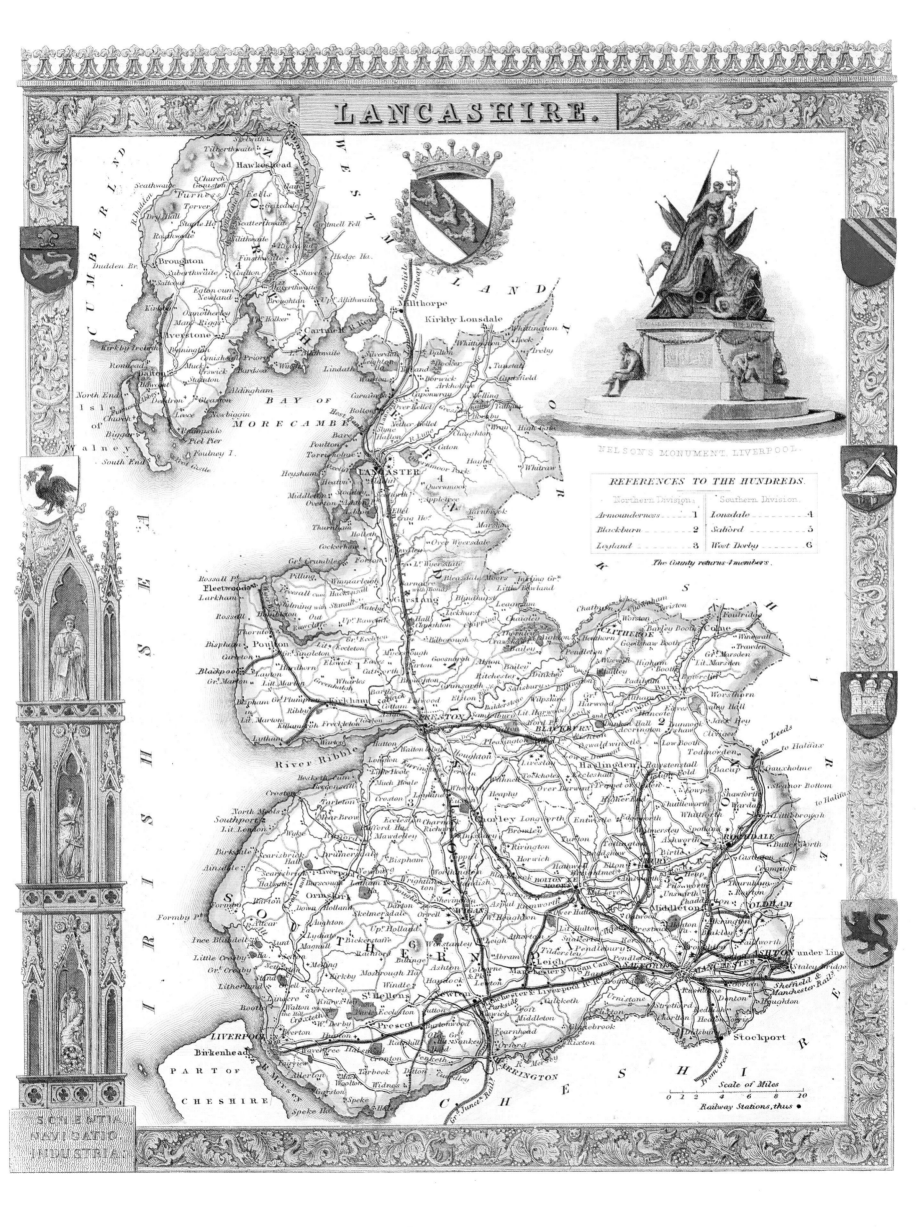

LANCASHIRE.

NELSON'S MONUMENT, LIVERPOOL.

REFERENCES TO THE HUNDREDS.

Northern Division.		Southern Division.	
Armounderness	1	Lonsdale	4
Blackburn	2	Salford	5
Leyland	3	West Derby	6

The County returns 4 members.

Scale of Miles

0 2 4   6   8   10

Railway Stations, thus ●

SCIENTIA
NAVIGATIO
INDUSTRIA

Leicestershire

A county of England, bounded by Derbyshire, Nottinghamshire, Lincolnshire, Rutland, Northamptonshire, and Warwickshire. It extends about 40 miles in each direction. It is divided into 6 hundreds, which contain 12 market towns and 200 parishes; the air is healthy, and the soil, in general strong and stiff, composed of clay and marl, affords great quantities of rich grazing land, and is peculiarly fitted for the culture of beans. Toward the north west the Bardon Hills rise to a great height; and in their neighbourhood lies Charnwood Forest, a rough and open tract. Farther to the north west are valuable coal-mines. The north eastern parts feed great numbers of sheep, which are the largest, and have the greatest fleeces of wool, of any in England; they are without horns, and clothed with thick long flakes of soft wool, particularly fitted for the worsted manufactures. The east and south eastern part of the county is a rich grazing tract. This county has been long famous for its large black dray-horses, of which great numbers are continually sent up to London, as well as for its horned cattle, and sheep, which supply the London markets with the largest mutton. The manufacture of stockings is the principal one in this county. Its chief rivers are the Avon, the Soar, anciently the Leire, the Wreke, Anker, Swift, Eye, and Welland. Leicester is its chief town. Population, 215,867. It returns 6 members to parliament.

LEICESTER

It is an ancient place, and though declined from its former magnitude, is still a large but not a handsome town. It contains 5 churches, near one of which are the famous ruins of a Roman wall. Here is also a Roman milliary, (or mile-stone), which forms the centre of an obelisk in one of the principal streets. The hall and kitchen of its ancient castle are still entire. The former is lofty and spacious, and the courts of justice, at the assizes, are held in them. One of its gateways also remains, with a very curious arch, the tower over which is now turned into a magazine for the county militia. Here is a very spacious market-place, with one of the largest markets in England for corn and cattle. The combing and spinning of wool into worsted, and manufacturing it into stockings, is the chief business of the town and neighbourhood. Its fairs, which are upon a large scale, for sheep, horses for the collar, cattle, cheese, &c., are on May 12th, July 5th, October 10th, and December 8th. It is seated on the river Soar, which has been made navigable from Leicester to Loughborough. It is 99 miles from London. Market, Saturday. Population, 48,167.

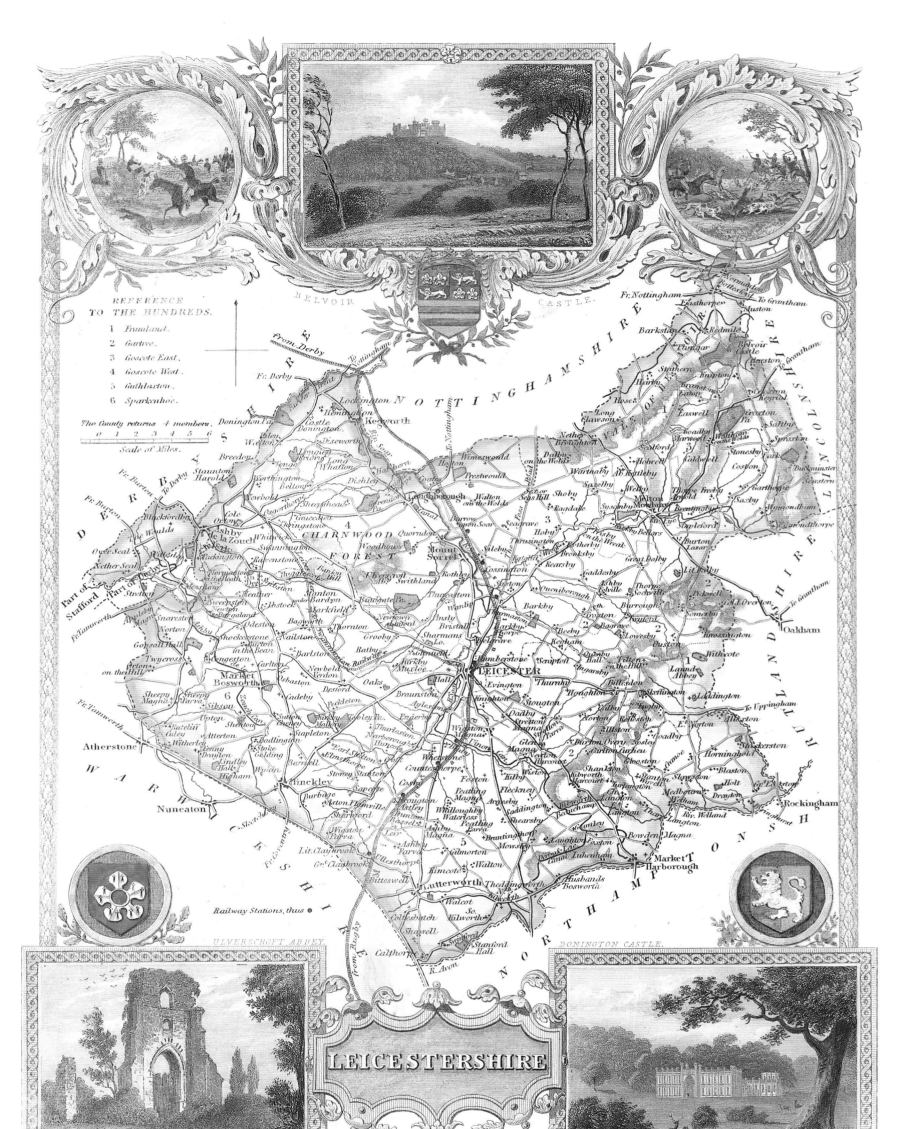

LEICESTERSHIRE

Lincolnshire

A county of England, lying on the German Ocean, and bounded by Norfolk, Cambridgeshire, Northamptonshire, Rutland, Leicestershire, Nottinghamshire, and Yorkshire. It is 77 miles in length, and 48 in breadth where widest. It is divided into three parts, namely Holland on the south east, Kesteven on the south west, and Lindsey on the north. It contains 30 hundreds, 1 city, 33 market towns, and 630 parishes. Its principal rivers are the Trent, Humber, Witham, Welland, Ancam, Nen, and Dun. The air is various, according to its three grand divisions. The soil in many places is very rich, the inland part producing corn in great plenty, and the fens cole-seed, and very rich pastures; whence their breed of cattle is larger than that of any other county in England except Somersetshire; their horses are also excellent, and very large; and their sheep are not only of the largest breed, but are clothed with a long thick wool, peculiarly fitted for the worsted and coarse woollen manufactures. It has some manufactures also. Population, 362,602. It sends 13 members to parliament.

Lincoln

Lincoln was formerly called Nicol. This city is pleasantly seated on the side of a hill, on the Witham, which here divides itself into three small channels. It is much reduced from its former extent and splendour, (when it contained 52 parish churches, and was one of the most populous cities of England, and a mart for all goods coming by land or water,) and now consists principally of one street, above 2 miles long, well paved, and several cross and parallel streets well peopled. Here are some handsome modern buildings, but more antique ones. The Romans' northgate still remains under the name of Newport Gate. It is a vast semicircle of stones, of very large dimensions, laid without mortar, and connected only by their uniform shape. The cathedral is a stately Gothic pile, one of the largest in England, and stands on so lofty a hill, that it may be seen 50 miles to the north and 30 to the south, and is particularly admired for its interior architecture, which is in the richest and lightest Gothic style. The famous bell, called Tom of Lincoln, is surpassed in magnitude by only two others in England. The chief trade here is in coals brought by the Trent and Fossdyke; and oats and wool, which are sent by the river Witham. It is 129 miles from London. Markets, Tuesday and Friday. Population, 16,172.

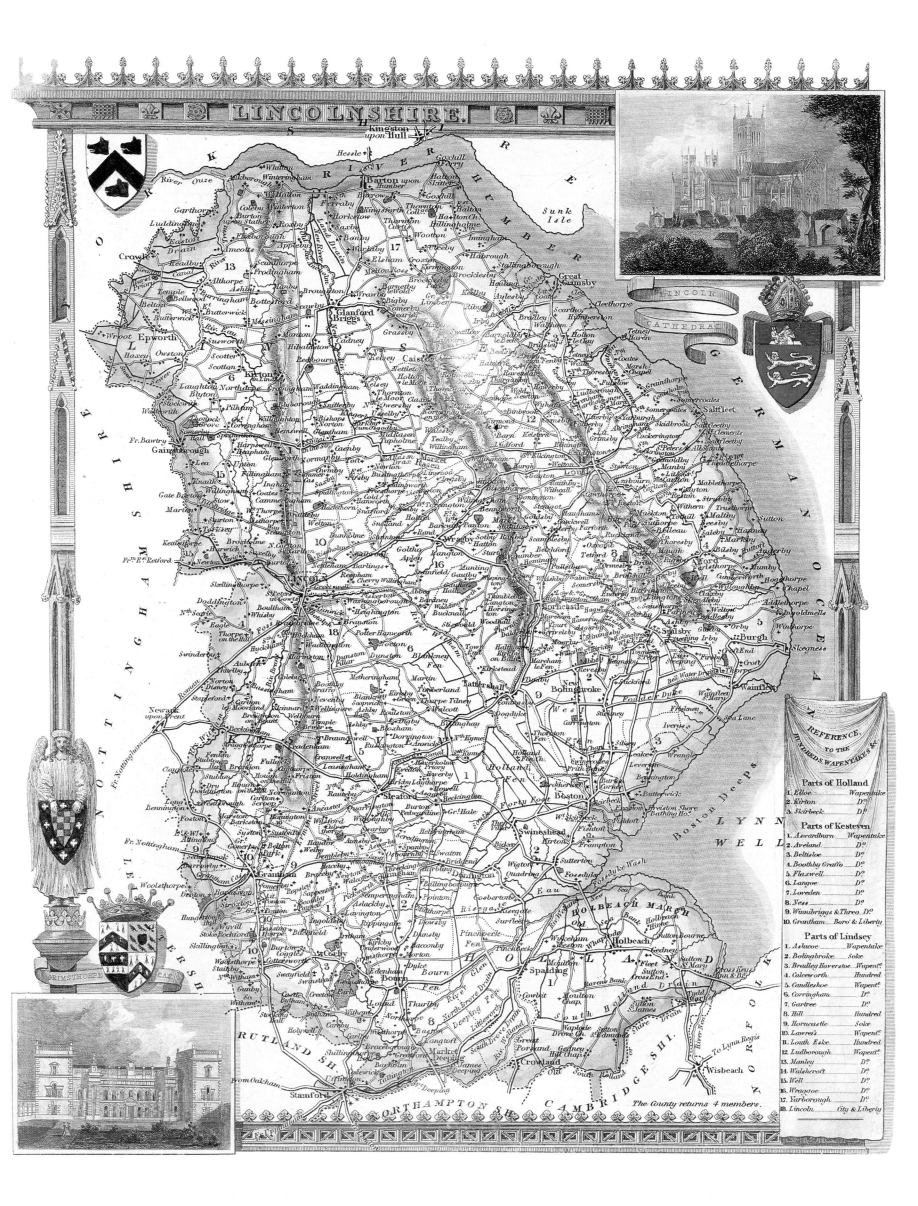

LINCOLNSHIRE.

LINCOLN CATHEDRAL

GRIMSTHORPE

REFERENCE.
TO THE
HUNDREDS WAPENTAKES &c.

Parts of Holland
1. Elloe   Wapentake
2. Kirton   D°
3. Skirbeck   D°

Parts of Kesteven
1. Awardburn   Wapentake
2. Aveland   D°
3. Beltisloe   D°
4. Boothby Graffo   D°
5. Flaxwell   D°
6. Langoe   D°
7. Loveden   D°
8. Ness   D°
9. Winnibriggs & Threo   D°
10. Grantham   Boro' & Liberty

Parts of Lindsey
1. Aslacoe   Wapentake
2. Bolingbroke   Soke
3. Bradley Haverstoe   Wapent.
4. Calceworth   Hundred
5. Candleshoe   Wapent.
6. Corringham   D°
7. Gartree   D°
8. Hill   Hundred
9. Horncastle   Soke
10. Lawress   Wapent.
11. Louth Eske   Hundred
12. Ludborough   Wapent.
13. Manley   D°
14. Walshcroft   D°
15. Well   D°
16. Wraggoe   D°
17. Yarborough   D°
18. Lincoln   City & Liberty

The County returns 4 members.

Boston

It is commodiously seated on both sides of the river Witham, over which it has a handsome high cast-iron bridge; by means of which river, assisted by navigable canals, it carries on a considerable inland trade. It also trades with London and the Baltic. It is a large, handsome town, with a spacious market-place; and a fine church, whose tower, 300 feet high, serves as a land-mark for sailors. It is 116 miles from London. Markets, Wednesday and Saturday. Population, 12,942.

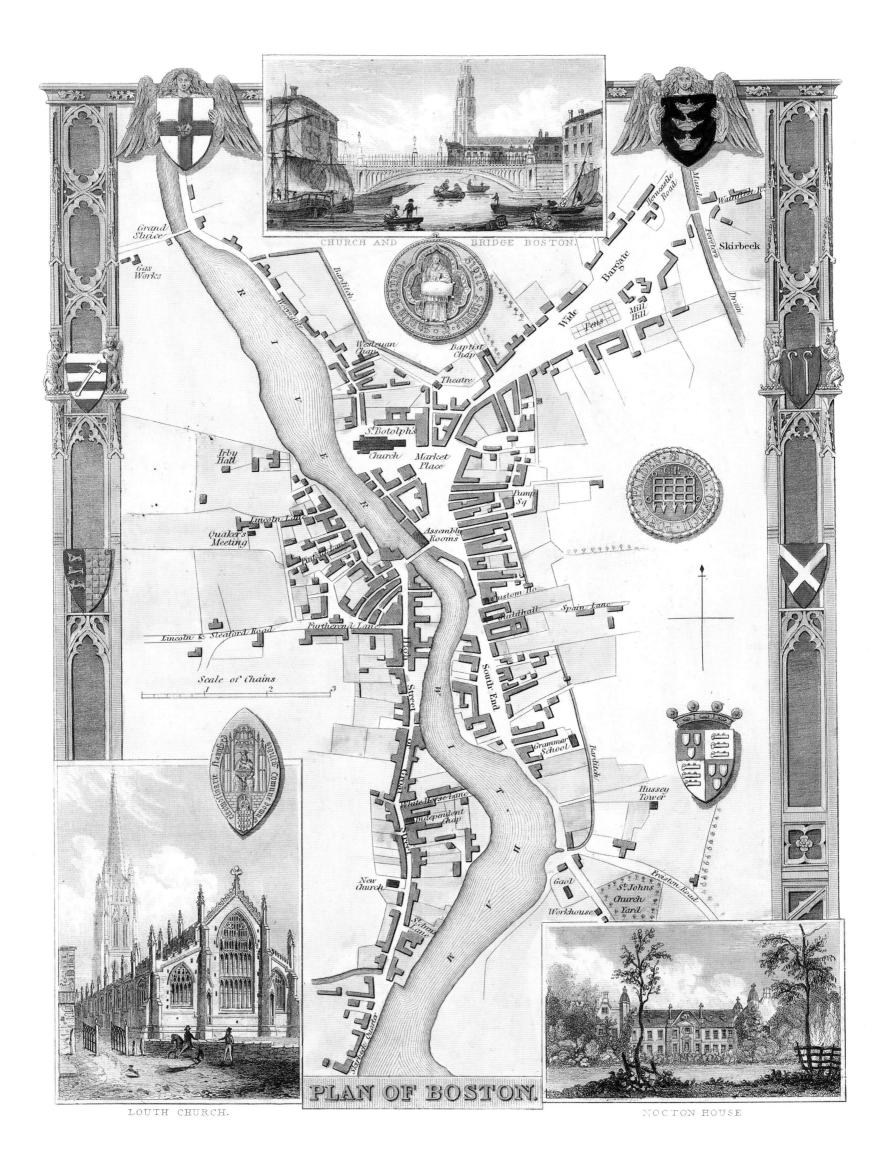

CHURCH AND BRIDGE BOSTON.

Grand Sluice

Gas Works

Bargate

Wide

Pens

Mill Hill

Hawcastle Road

Skirbeck

Drain

Marsh

Wainfleet Rd

Forsters

Bargate

Wesleyan Chap.

Baptist Chap.

Theatre

S.t Botolph's Church

Market Place

Irby Hall

Pump Sq.

Quaker's Meeting

Lincoln Lane

Pinfold Lane

Assembly Rooms

Custom Ho.

Guildhall

Span Lane

Lincoln & Sleaford Road

Furtherend Lane

South End

Scale of Chains

Grammar School

Bargate

White Horse Lane

Independent Chap.

Hussey Tower

New Church

S.t Ann's Lane

Gaol

Workhouse

S.t Johns Church Yard

Braston Road

Skirbeck Quarter

PLAN OF BOSTON.

LOUTH CHURCH.

NOCTON HOUSE

Isle of Man

Man is an island of Great Britain, in the Irish Sea, about 30 miles in length, and from 8 to 15 in breadth. It is very hilly, and one of its heights exceeds 2000 feet. It has mines of lead, iron, and copper, and quarries of building stone and slate. The soil varies in different tracts, yet produces more corn than is sufficient to maintain the natives. The air, which is sharp and cold in winter, is healthy, and the inhabitants live to a very great age. The commodities of this island are small black cattle and horses, wool, fine and coarse linen, hides, skins, honey, tallow, and herrings. About the rocks of the island breeds an incredible number of all sorts of sea-fowl, and especially on the Calf of Man, a small island not far from its most southerly point. The language is a dialect of the Erse. In its civil government, which is peculiar to it, the island is divided into six sheedings, each having its proper coroner, who is intrusted with the peace of his district, and acts in the nature of a sheriff. The House of Keys is its elective legislature, &c. Castle Town is its chief place. Population, 47,975.

CASTLETOWN

The principal place of the Isle of Man, with a strong, beautiful castle, of free-stone, still entire. At the entrance is a great stone chair for the governor, and two smaller ones for the deemsters; and beyond this court is a room where the keys sit. On the other side are seen the governor's house, the chancery offices, and good barracks. It is situated on the south eastern point of the island, with a shallow, rocky harbour. Population, 2283. Latitude 54.2 North. Longitude 4.35 West.

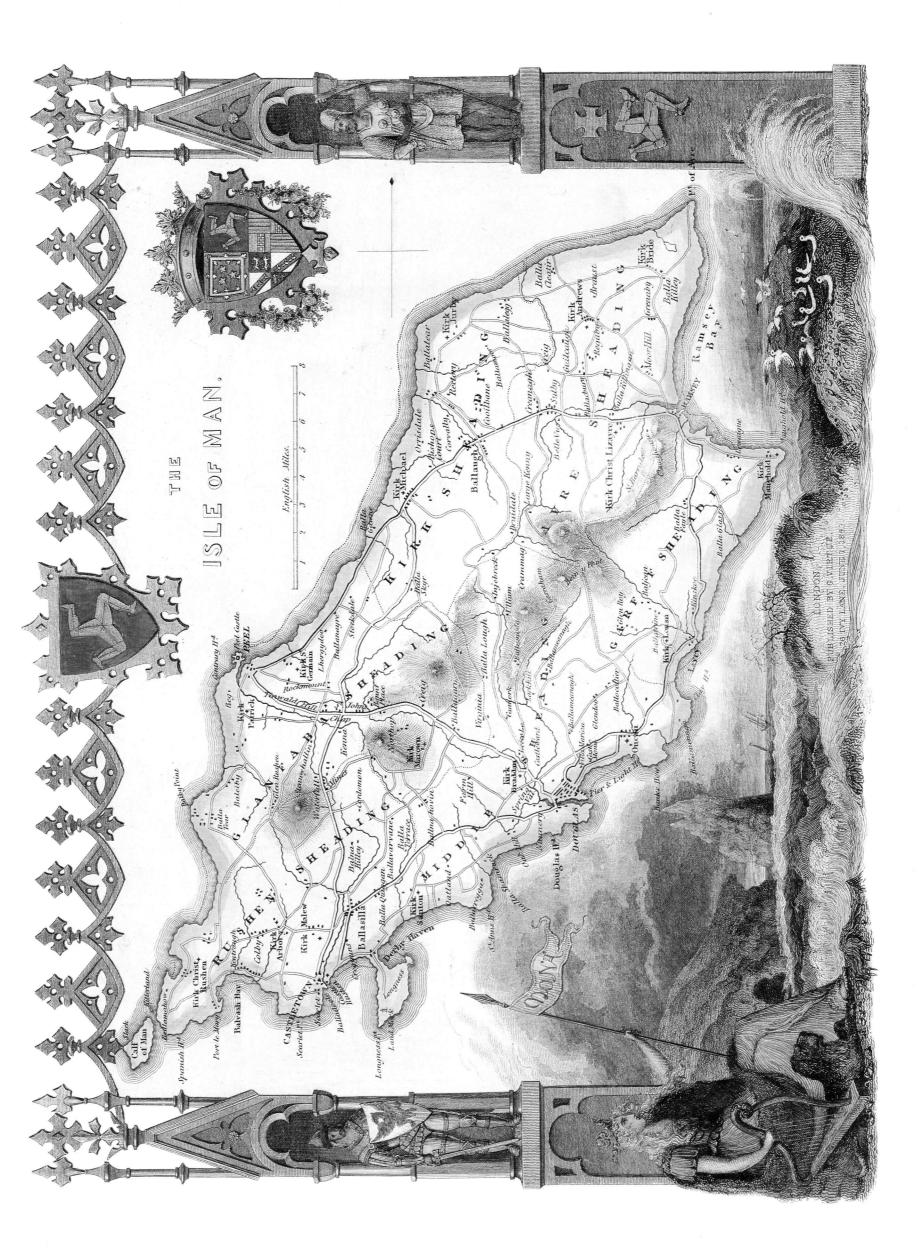

THE
ISLE OF MAN.

English Miles.
1 2 3 4 5 6 7 8

KIRK SHEADING

AYRE SHEADING

GARFF SHEADING

GLANFABA SHEADING

MICHAEL SHEADING

MIDDLE SHEADING

RUSHEN SHEADING

PEEL

CASTLETOWN

DOUGLAS

Ramsey Bay

MAN

LONDON
PUBLISHED BY J. & F. TALLIS,
29 IVY LANE, JUNE 11, 1843.

Middlesex

A county of England, bounded by Hertfordshire, Essex, Surrey, Kent, and Buckinghamshire. It is one of the least counties in England, being only about 22 miles in length, and 14 in breadth. It contains 7 market towns, and about 98 parishes, without including those in London and Westminster. The air is healthy; but the soil in general being a lean gravel, it is naturally a district of little fertility, though by means of the vicinity to the metropolis, many parts of it are converted into rich beds of manure, clothed with almost perpetual verdure. Besides the Thames, the Lea, and the Coln, Middlesex is watered by several small streams, one of which, called the New River, is artificially brought from Amwell, in Hertfordshire, for the purpose of supplying London with water. Indeed, the whole county may be considered as a demesne to the metropolis, the land being laid out in gardens, pastures, and enclosures of all sorts, for its convenience and support. London is its chief place, and county town. Population, 1,576,636.

WESTMINSTER

It stands on the Thames, and forms part of the English metropolis. In it are situated the Houses of Parliament, the great government offices, the chief law courts, &c. Its Abbey is one of the most magnificent of our collegiate churches, and is the British Walhalla. Population, 222,053.

THAMES

The largest river of England, which rises in the Cotswold Hills, Gloucestershire; and, receiving the waters of many smaller streams, flows, after a course of 215 miles, into the German Ocean between Kent and Essex.

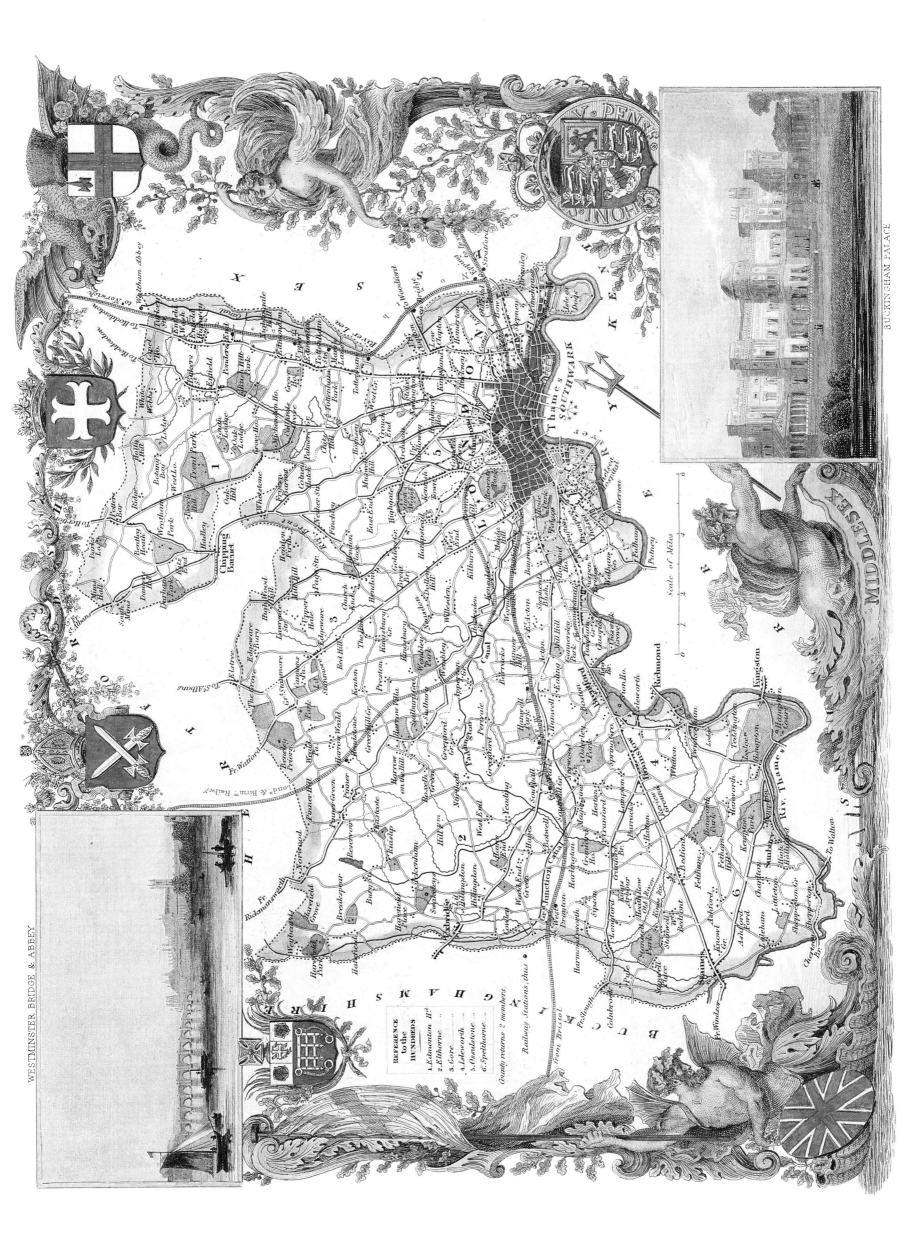

MIDDLESEX

BUCKINGHAM PALACE

WESTMINSTER BRIDGE & ABBEY

REFERENCE
to the
HUNDREDS
1. Edmonton Hd.
2. Elthorne
3. Gore
4. Iseleworth
5. Ossulstone
6. Spelthorne

Railway Stations, thus ....
County returns 2 members.

Scale of Miles

London

The metropolis of the United Kingdom of Great Britain and Ireland stands on the Thames, which is crossed by eight bridges, and under which a tunnel has been driven; extends from Woolwich and Bow to Fulham and Hammersmith, and from Highgate to Norwood, including the cities of London and Westminster, with their liberties, and the towns, parishes, &c. &c. which cover this vast area. The streets of the city, with the exception of the great thoroughfares, are for the most part narrow and irregular; but the main lines of traffic and communication are wide and noble, as are the more recently built parts of this enormous city.

The public edifices are innumerable, and for magnificence may vie with those of any city in the world. St. Paul's Cathedral stands pre-eminent amongst these, built by Sir Christopher Wren which, though it is most disadvantageously situated, being closely surrounded by houses, and is said not to have been the edifice Sir Christopher had hoped to raise, is yet sufficiently imposing in appearance. Many of the other churches are very noble buildings, but most of them are in by-streets, and scarcely any are built on the Gothic model, which prevails throughout the country, some of them, even, being express imitations of Roman and Grecian temples. Some of the places of worship belonging to other communions are fine structures. Of the government and public buildings, the New Palace of Westminster, the remains of Whitehall, the Horse-guards, Admiralty, and other connected public offices; the Post-Office, the Royal Exchange, the Mansion House, the Custom House, Somerset House, the India House, Lincoln's Inn Buildings, and those of the Temple and other Inns of Court; the British Museum, the Bank (for the notion of complete security against unauthorized ingress,) the prisons of Newgate, Coldbath-fields &c., (for the notion of equal security against unauthorized egress,) the National Gallery, (for the exhibition of no notion at all,) University College, Christ's Hospital, the Theatres, the Colosseum, the Hospitals, the Bazaars, the Railway Termini, deserve special notice and mention.

Whilst the club houses of the West End, the companies' halls of the city, and many private residences of the nobility and gentry, and the inns, vie with them in magnificence. The bridges, particularly London, Waterloo, and Hungerford bridges, are very noble structures. The Queen's Palace in St. James's Park, is chiefly noted for the marble arch and splendid bronze gates. Temple Bar, which obstructs the junction of the Strand and Fleet Street, is a relic of the past; as are the Tower, with its armouries and other marvels, sadly curtailed, and London Stone, said to be the central *lapis miliaris* of Roman Britain.

Yet perhaps these are not, though they first meet the eye, the most astonishing features of the British metropolis. The prodigious docks, with their immense bonding-warehouses, the warehouses of the city, towering into the air, and sinking deeply into the earth, convey the notion of wealth and commerce completely stupendous. Vast manufactories of almost all kinds of commodities, which are

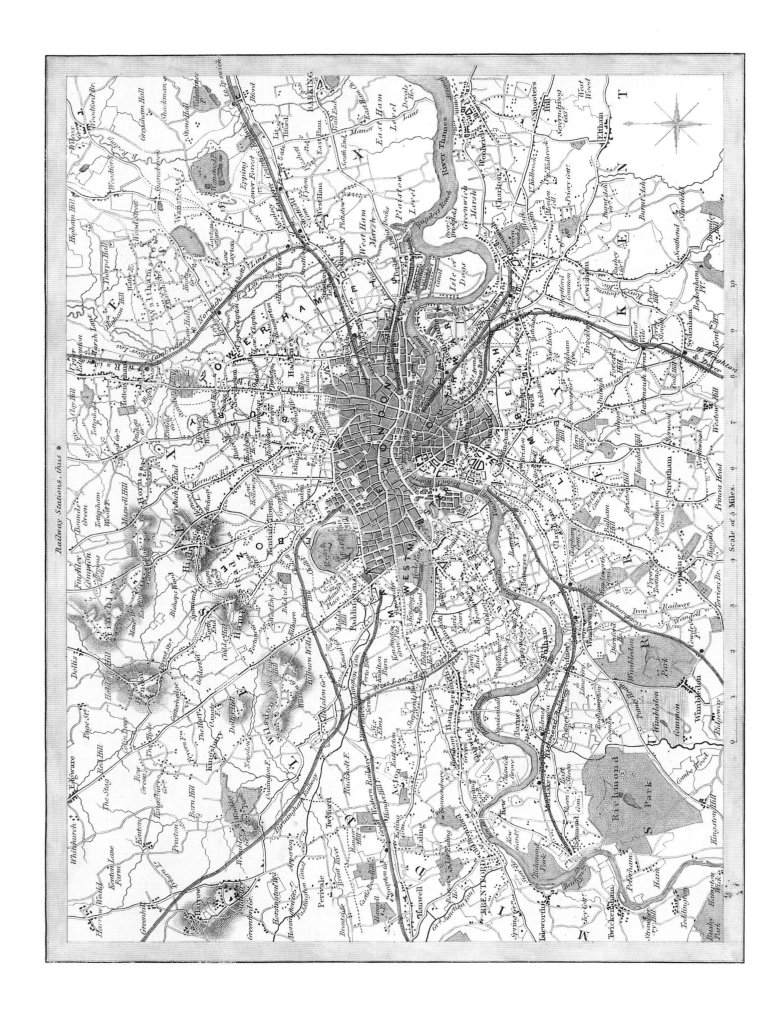

hardly recognised in the endless crowds of buildings, make London, in this respect, the rival of whole provinces. By means of the river, London ranks as the first port of the kingdom; canals enable it to communicate, for the transit of heavy goods, with all the interior of the country; whilst railways, branching out in every direction, bring the remotest counties into closest proximity with this emporium of the world, for goods of more perishable character or lighter carriage, and for travellers. Here are six parks, (including Greenwich Park,) which are open to the public. The squares, which are usually ornamentally planted, are of great advantage to some districts, in regard to health. But the parts of the metropolis inhabited by the poorer classes, are yet the prolific sources of disease; and the retention of Smithfield market and the slaughter-houses in the very heart of London must also be noticed as a heavy drawback on the health, safety, and even morality of the city.

For every species of rational and intelligent recreation, London stands pre-eminent; theatres, concert-rooms, museums, lecture-rooms, scientific institutions, ranging from the Royal Society down to the District Mechanics' Institute, &c., offering a wide and unequalled diversity of most instructive amusement. Unhappily, it is equally unrivalled for affording all that can pollute, and degrade, and destroy.

London is also the centre of the literary world; not only are the chief newspapers, and monthly and quarterly books, whose authors hope for any sale, also. Of the numberless charitable and religious institutions it is impossible to make any mention. The city of London is under the control of a corporation, of enormous wealth; whose practical inefficiency, and steadfast resistance of all reformation or change, are matters of painful notoriety. Several regiments of cavalry and infantry are customarily quartered in or near the metropolis but chiefly for state purposes, and occasions of royal pomp; the guardianship of the streets and the public peace and safety are committed to a numerous and well-appointed body of police. The whole of the district is also well lighted with gas, and well supplied with spring water, by various companies. Population, London (within the walls), 54,626; (without the walls), 70,382. Total metropolitan, 1,873,676. Latitude 51.31 North. Longitude 0.6 West.

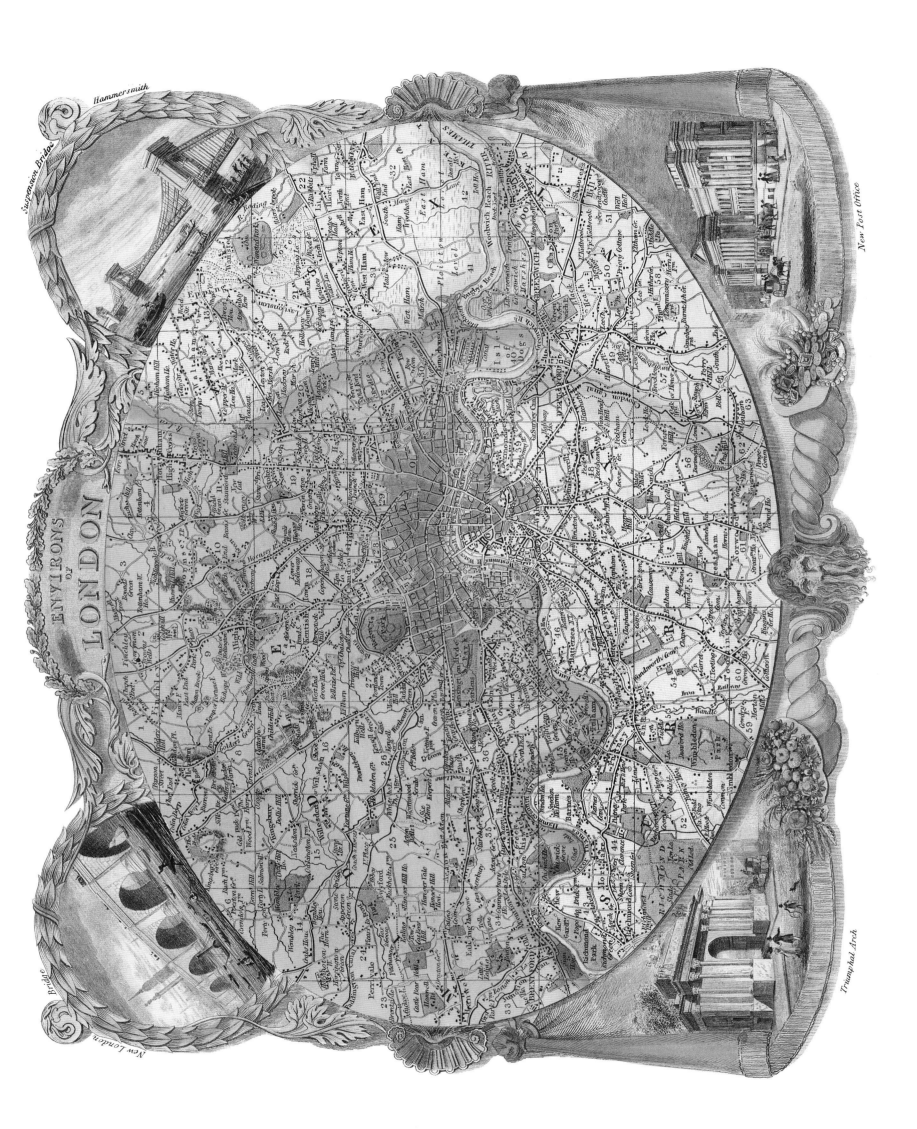

ENVIRONS OF LONDON

Suspension Bridge

Hammersmith

New London Bridge

New Post Office

Triumphal Arch

Monmouthshire

A county of England, lying on the Bristol Channel, and bounded by Herefordshire, Brecknockshire, Gloucestershire, and Glamorganshire. Its length is about 24 miles, and its breadth 21. It is divided into 6 hundreds, and contains 7 market towns, and 127 parishes. The air is temperate and healthy, and the soil fruitful, though mountainous and woody. The hills feed sheep, goats, and horned cattle, and the valleys produce plenty of grass and corn. Beside the Wye, the Munnow, and the Rhyney, or Rumney, this county has almost peculiar to itself the river Usk, which divides it into two unequal portions, the eastern and largest part of which is a tract fertile, on the whole, in corn and pastures, and well wooded. It abounds with limestone, which is burnt on the spot, for the general manure of the country. The smaller western portion is mountainous, and in great part unfavourable for cultivation; whence it is devoted to the feeding of sheep. It has several long narrow valleys, watered by streams that fall into the Bristol Channel. All the rivers above-mentioned, particularly the Wye and Usk, abound with fish, especially salmon and trout. Monmouthshire was formerly reckoned one of the counties of Wales, but since the reign of Charles II, it has been considered as an English county. The people use the Welsh language, but the English tongue is coming into use. The manufacture of this county is flannels. Monmouth is its county town. Population, 134,355. It sends 4 members to parliament.

MONMOUTH

It is pleasantly seated at the confluence of the rivers Wye, Munnow, and Trothy, which almost surround it. It is a large handsome town, and carries on a considerable trade with Bristol by the Wye. It had once a stately castle, the remains of which show it to have been very strong. It is 128 miles from London. Market for corn and provisions, Saturday. Fairs on Whitsun-Tuesday, September 4th, and November 22nd. Population, 5446.

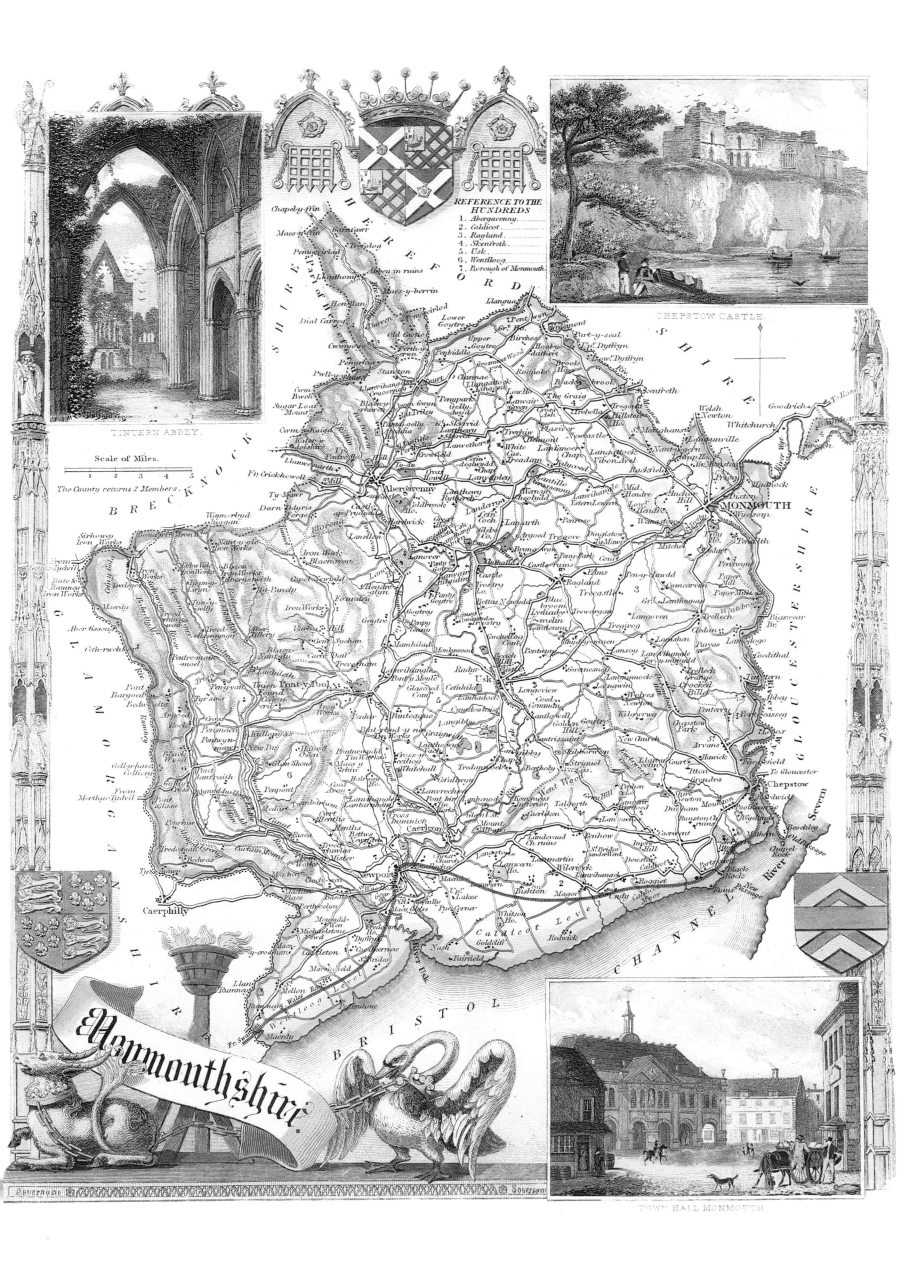

TINTERN ABBEY.

REFERENCE TO THE
HUNDREDS
1. Abergavenny.
2. Caldicot.
3. Ragland.
4. Skenfreth.
5. Usk.
6. Wentlloog.
7. Borough of Monmouth.

CHEPSTOW CASTLE.

Scale of Miles.
1 2 3 4 5

The County returns 2 Members.

HEREFORDSHIRE

BRECKNOCKSHIRE

GLAMORGANSHIRE

MONMOUTH

Abergavenny

Usk

Pont-y-Pool

Caerleon

Newport

Chepstow

GLOUCESTERSHIRE

Caerphilly

Monmouthshire

BRISTOL CHANNEL

River Severn

TOWN HALL MONMOUTH.

Norfolk

A county of England, lying on the German Ocean; bounded by Cambridgeshire, Lincolnshire, and Suffolk. It extends 70 miles in length and 40 in breadth. It contains 33 hundreds, 1 city, 32 market towns, and 660 parishes. The face of this county varies less than in most tracts of equal extent in England. Not one hill of any considerable height is to be seen in the whole county; yet, in most parts, its surface is broken into gentle swells and depressions. At the western extremity is a considerable tract of flat fenny land, which is part of the Bedford Level; and, on the east, a narrow tract of marshes runs from the sea, near Yarmouth, to some distance up the country. Between Lincolnshire and the western extremity, is a broad but shallow arm of the sea, called the Wash. The south western part is very sandy and light land, not very easy nor profitable for husbandry; but the rest is a good mixed soil, generally very productive in corn of all kinds, mangold-wurzel, turnips, &c. Excellent butter and cheese is made, especially in the marshlands, and is sold in London as Cambridge butter and Stilton cheese. Cattle, sheep, fowls, &c. are abundant. Game and rabbits are too plentiful by far for the farmers. A few bustards yet live in the western parts. On the sea-coast, herrings and mackerel are caught in great plenty; and Yarmouth, in particular, is noted for the curing of red herrings. The air of this county is sharp and piercing, which throws the seasons more backward than in other counties under the same latitude; but it is very wholesome, particularly in the inland parts. Its principal rivers are the Great Ouse, Nen, Little Ouse, Waveney, Wensum, Yare, and Bure. Norwich is the capital. Population, 412,664. It sends 12 representatives to parliament.

NORWICH

It is an ancient, large, and populous city, seated on the river Wensum, which runs through it, and is navigable to Yarmouth, without locks. It has a stately ancient castle, on a hill, which commands a fine view of the city and surrounding country, and is used as the county gaol; and a fine cathedral, with a very lofty spire: here are also 2 good public libraries, a city and county hospital, a shire-hall, a handsome guild-hall, and a corn-hall. The ancient bridewell, now a private house, is built of flints, remarkable for being beautifully cut into regular little squares, without any visible cement. It had formerly 60 churches, &c., and has now 36 churches, beside the cathedral, chapels, and dissenting meeting-houses. It was formerly a great manufacturing city; but it has much declined of late. Norwich has 10 bridges over the Wensum, and is the centre of several important lines of railways. The provision market is a fine square, and is well supplied. It is 108 miles from London. Markets, Wednesday and Saturday. Population, 62,344.

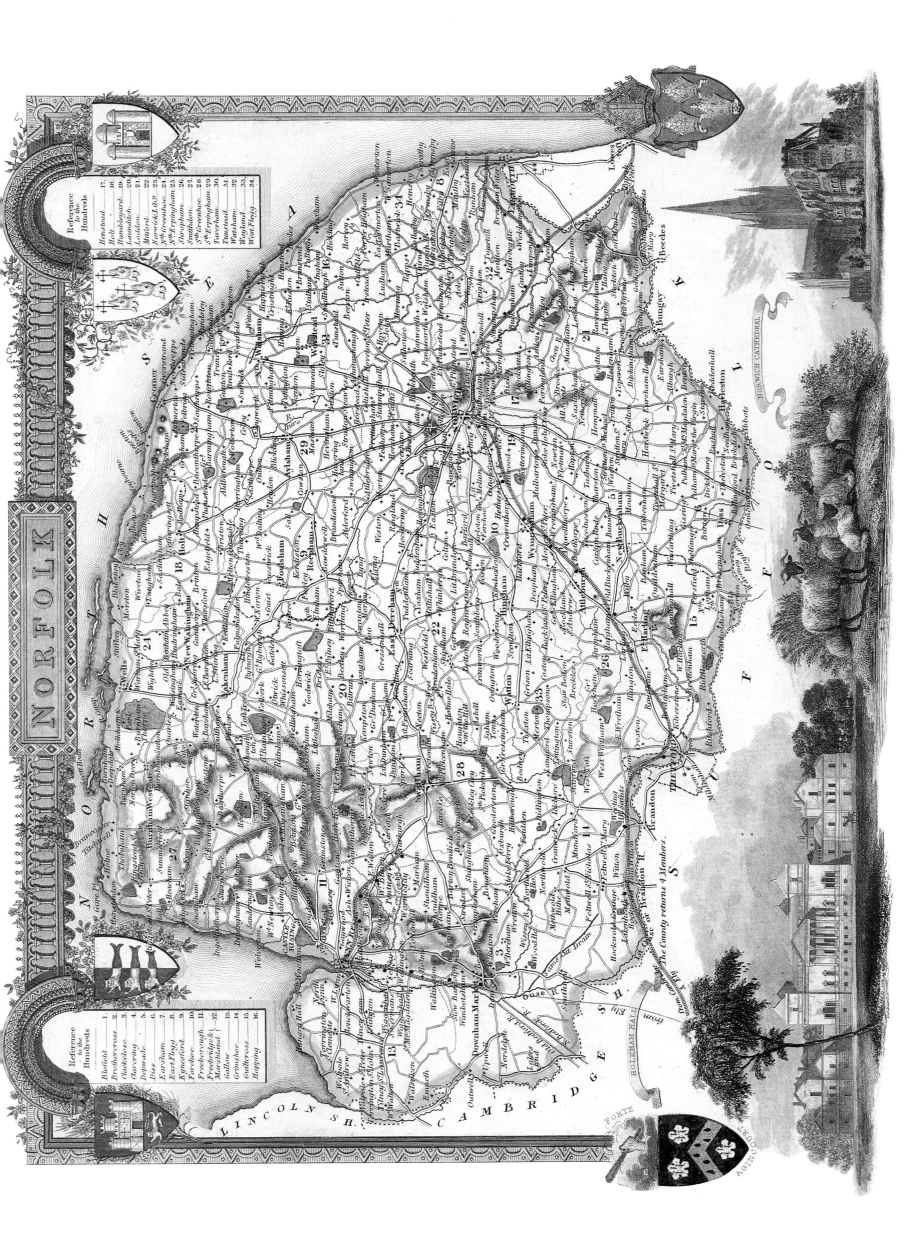

NORFOLK

NORWICH CATHEDRAL

HOLKHAM HALL

The County returns 4 Members.

Northamptonshire

A county of England, bounded by Leicestershire, Rutlandshire, Lincolnshire, the counties of Cambridge, Huntingdon, and Bedford, Buckinghamshire, Oxfordshire, and Warwickshire. It is divided into 20 hundreds, containing a city, 13 market towns, and 336 parishes. The air of this county is very healthy, except in the north eastern part near Peterborough, which being surrounded and intersected by rivers, is very liable to inundations, and forms the commencement of the fenny tract extending to the Lincolnshire Washes. It is a fine and pleasant county, and possesses some considerable remains of its old forests, particularly those of Rockingham in the north west, and of Salcey and Whittlebury in the south. In this last wild cats are still found. The products of this county are, in general, the same as those of other farming countries. It is, indeed, peculiarly celebrated for grazing land; that tract, especially, which lies from Northampton northward to the Leicestershire border. Horned cattle and other animals are here fed to extraordinary sizes, and many horses of the large black breed are reared. Woad for the dyers is cultivated in this part; but the county is not distinguished for manufactures, excepting the trifling one of bone lace. The principal rivers are the Nen and Welland; beside which it is partly watered by the Ouse, Leam, Cherwell, and Avon. The county town is Northampton. Population, 199,228. It sends 8 members to parliament.

NORTHAMPTON

It is seated on an eminence, gently sloping to the river Nen, which is joined here by another rivulet, and has been made navigable to Lynn. Its principal manufacture is that of boots and shoes, of which many are made here, and in other parts of the county, for exportation. Some stockings and lace are also made here. The horse-fairs of this place are reckoned to exceed all others in the kingdom. It is a handsome, well-built town, and has a regular, spacious market-place, one of the finest in England, a good free-school, and a county infirmary and gaol. Within half a mile of Northampton is a fine Gothic structure, called Queen's Cross, erected by Edward I in memory of his queen Eleanor. It is 66 miles from London. Markets, Wednesday, Friday, and Saturday. Fairs, on February 20, April 15, May 4, August 5, and 26, September 19, November 28, and December 19. Population, 21,242.

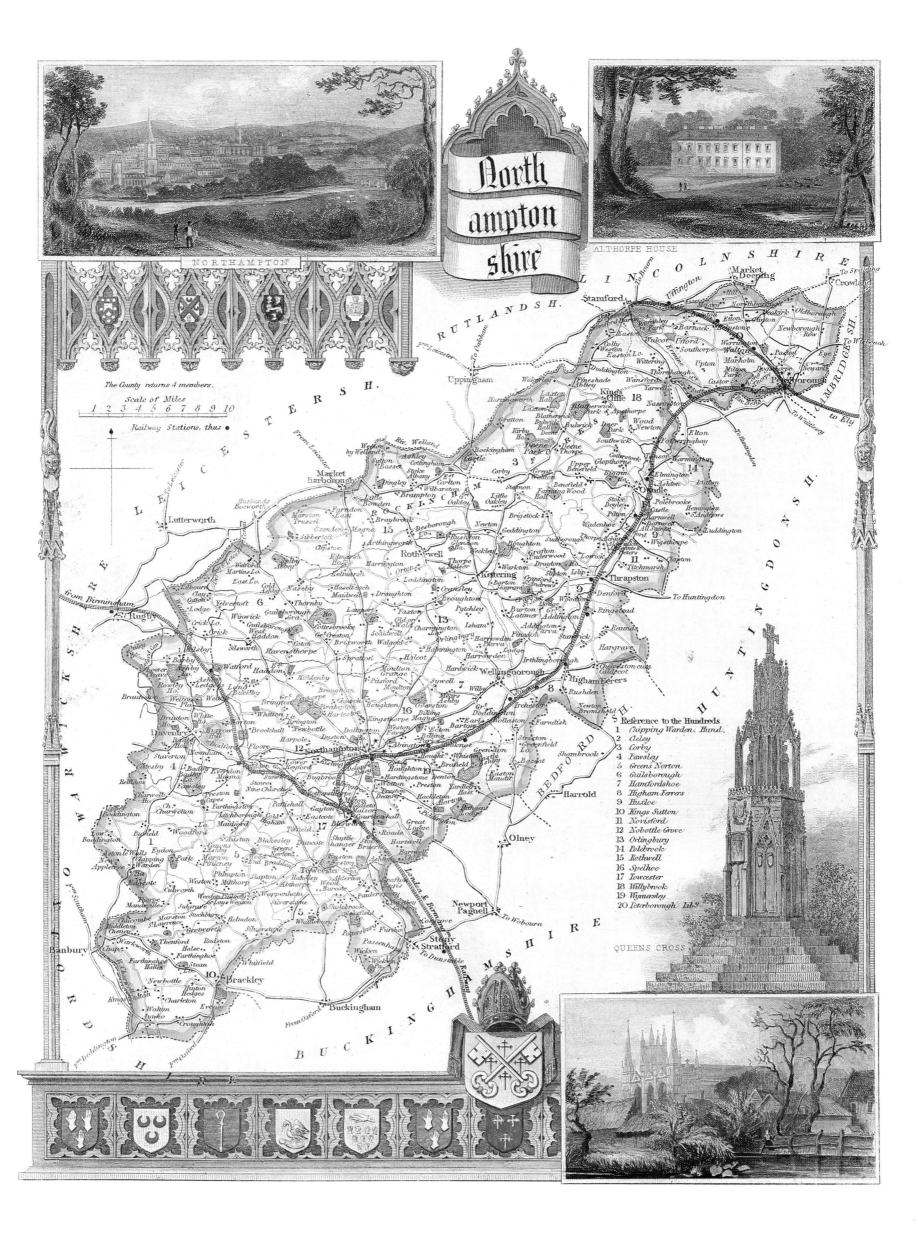

Northumberland

The most northerly county of England. It lies next to Scotland, on the German Ocean, and is bounded by Durham and Cumberland. It extends about 70 miles in length, and 50 in breadth; and contains 12 market towns, and 460 parishes. The air is not so cold as might be imagined from the latitude in which it lies; and the snow seldom lies long in Northumberland, except on the tops of the hills, some of which are above 2000 feet high. The soil is various; the eastern part being fruitful, having very good wheat and most sorts of corn, with rich meadows on the banks of the rivers; but the western part is generally barren, it being mostly heathy and mountainous. It yields lead; and is one of the most productive and best coal-fields in England. Iron and glass-works are its principal manufactories; and it has some fisheries. This county is well watered by rivers, the principal of which are the Tyne, Tweed, and Coquet. Alnwick is the county-town, but the largest and richest is Newcastle. Population, 250,278. It returns 8 members to parliament.

Alnwick

Alnwick is the county town of Northumberland, 310 miles from London. Seated on the little river Alne, it is populous and well built. It has a fine market square, surrounded with piazzas. One of the old gates is still standing. There is an ancient castle near it, the seat of the Duke of Northumberland. Market, Saturday. Population, 6626.

Newcastle

Or Newcastle-upon-Tyne. It is situated among steep hills, on the Tyne, which is here a fine and deep river; so that ships of 3 or 4 hundred tons burden may safely come up to the town, though the large colliers are stationed at Shields. It is a very secure haven, and is defended by Clifford's Fort, which effectually commands all vessels that enter the river. The town may be considered as divided into two parts, of which Gateshead, on the Durham side, is one; and both are joined by a fine stone bridge consisting of 9 arches. The town rises on the north bank of the river, where the streets upon the ascent are exceedingly steep. Many of the houses are built of stone, but some of them are timber, and the rest of brick. The castle, which is old and ruinous, overlooks the whole town. The exchange, church-houses, and other public buildings, are elegant; and the quay for landing goods is long and large. Here is a hall for the surgeons, a large hospital, built by the contribution of the keel-men, for the maintenance of the poor of their fraternity; and several other charitable foundations. It is situated in the centre of the great collieries, which have for centuries supplied London, all the eastern, and some of the midland and southern parts of the kingdom with coal. This trade has been the source of great opulence to Newcastle; which, besides, exports large quantities of lead, salt, salmon, butter, tallow, and grindstones. Ships are sent hence to the Greenland fishery. It also possesses manufactories of steel, iron, and woollen cloth; and in the town and neighbourhood are several glass-houses. The streets in the old part of Newcastle are unsightly and narrow, but the newer parts are handsome and commodious. Newcastle is 270 miles from London. Markets, Tuesday and Saturday. Population, 49,860.

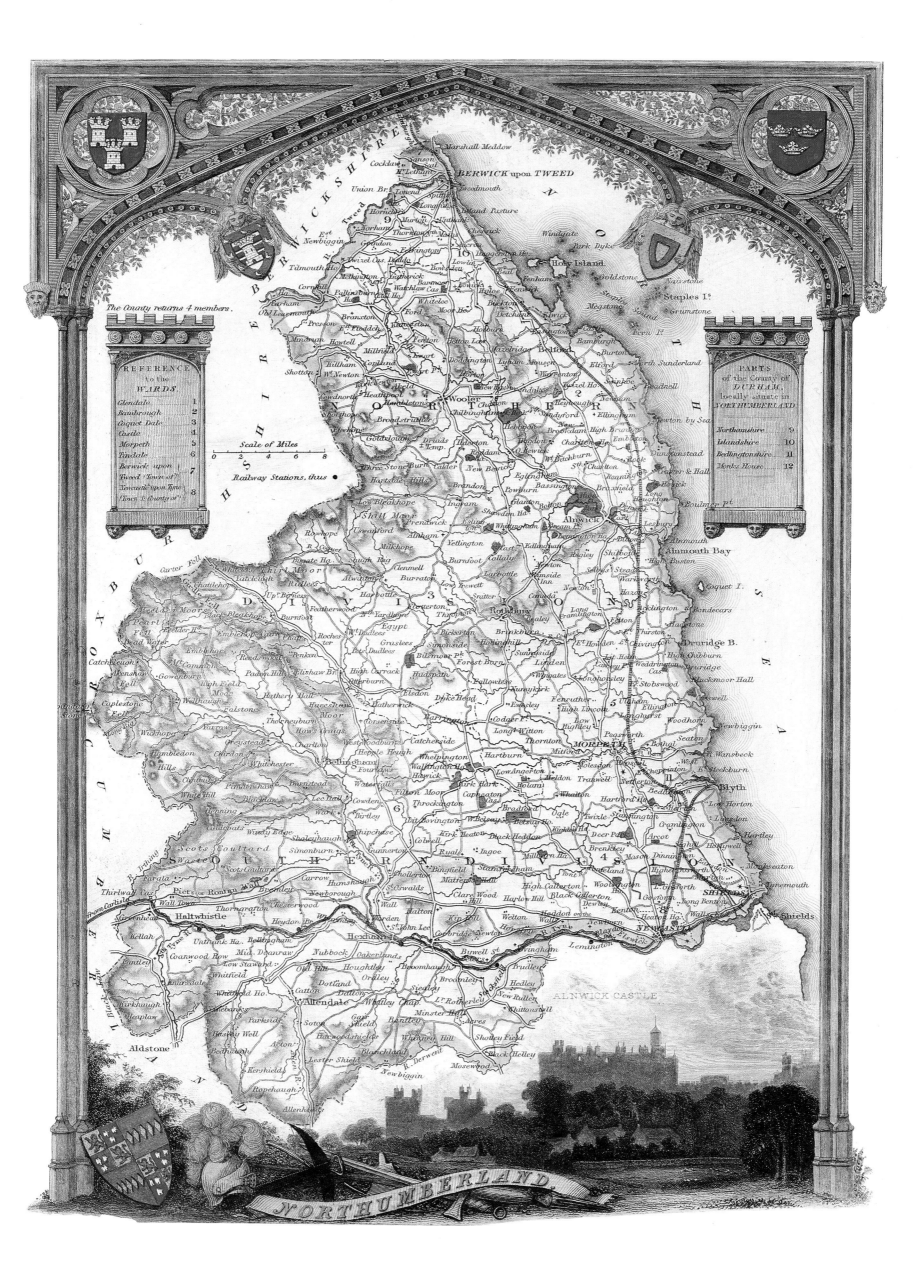

NORTHUMBERLAND

Nottinghamshire

A county of England, bounded by Yorkshire, Lincolnshire, Leicestershire, and Derbyshire. Its greatest length is 50 miles, its greatest breadth about 25. It is divided into 8 hundreds, and contains 13 towns and 168 parishes. The principal rivers are the Trent and Idle. Almost the whole of the middle and western parts of the county were formerly occupied by the extensive forest of Sherwood, which is the only royal forest north of the Trent; but the wood has in many parts been cleared, and the extent of the forest much contracted. The chief products of this county are corn, malt, pitcoal, of which there is great plenty. Their other commodities are malt, wool, liquorice, wood, fish, and fowl. Their manufactures chiefly consist of frame-work, knitting, glass, and earthenware. The principal town is Nottingham. Population, 249,910.

Nottingham

It is pleasantly seated on a rocky eminence, above the meadows bordering the Trent; on the highest part of which stands the castle, a large, elegant, and noble palace, belonging to the Duke of Newcastle, with a most extensive prospect. It is a large, populous, and handsome town, with a spacious market-place, and considered as one of the principal seats of the stocking manufacture, particularly of the finer kinds, as those of silk and cotton. It has also a manufactory of glass and coarse earthenware, and a considerable trade in malt. It is remarkable for its vaults or cellars cut in the rock. It is 125 miles from London. Markets, Wednesday and Saturday. Fairs, on Friday after January 13th, May 7th, Thursday before Easter, and October 2nd. Population, 53,091.

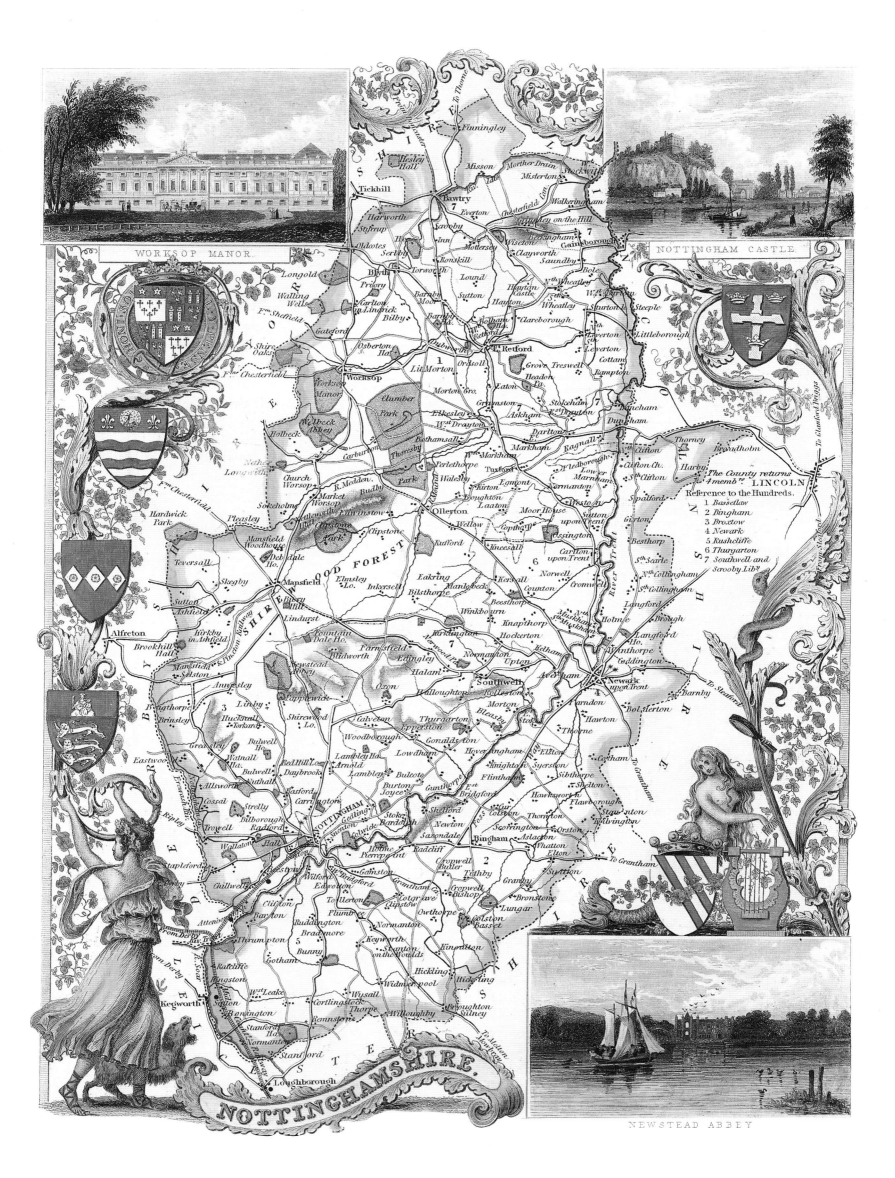

WORKSOP MANOR.

NOTTINGHAM CASTLE.

To Thorne
Finningley
Hesley Hall
Misson
Mother Drain
To Stockwith
Tickhill
Misterton
Bawtry
Harworth
Everton
Chesterfield Ca.
Gringley on the Hill
Styrrup
Scrooby
Inn
Walkeringham
Oldcotes
Serlby
Mattersey
Wiseton
Beckingham
Gainsborough
Blyth
Torworth
Lound
N.th Wheatley
W.st Burton
Priory
Barnby Moor
Sutton
Hayton
Clareborough
Steeple
Longold
Carlton Lindrick
Bilby
Barnby Ma.
Bolham
Clareborough
Sturton le
Walling Wells
Gateford
Clumber
Ranskill
Clayworth
Saundby
Bole
Fm Sheffield
Osberton Hall
Babworth
E.st Retford
Grove
Treswell
Cottam
Shire Oaks
Lit. Morton
Driscoll
Headon Ho.
Rampton
Fm Chesterfield
Worksop
Morten Gro.
Eaton
Pleasley
Worksop Manor
Elkesley
W.st Drayton
Askham
Dunham
Welbeck Abbey
Holbeck
Bothamsall
Thoresby
Markham
Ragnall
Thorney
Broadholm
Nether Langwith
Carburton
Walesby
Tuxford
Kirton
Egmont
S.th Clifton
Harby
LINCOLN
Church Worsop
R. Medden
Budby
Boughton
Normanton
Spalford
The County returns 4 memb.rs
Hardwick Park
Market Worsop
Edwinstow
Clipstone
Wellow
Laxton
Moor House
Sutton upon Trent
Reference to the Hundreds.
Teversall
Pleasley
Mansfield Woodhouse
Rufford
Kneesall
Carlton upon Trent
Besthorp
1 Bassetlaw
2 Bingham
Skegby
Debdale Ho.
Elmsley Lo.
Eakring
Kersall
Norwell
S.th Scarle
3 Broxtow
4 Newark
Sutton Ashfield
Mansfield
Inkersell
Bilsthorpe
Manlebeck
Beesthorp
Counton
Cromwell
N.th Collingham
5 Rushcliffe
6 Thurgarton
Kirkby in Ashfield
Lindurst
Winkbourn
Knapthorp
S.th Collingham
7 Southwell and Scrooby Lib.ty
Alfreton
Fountain Dale Ho.
Kirkington
Hockerton
Holme
Langford
Brookhill Hall
Blidworth
Farnsfield
Edingley
Normanton
Upton
Kelham
Langford Ho.
Brough
Mansfield Woodhouse
Newstead Abbey
Halam
Averham
Winthorpe
Coddington
Annesley
Oxton
Willoughton
Southwell
Newark upon Trent
Linby
Papplewick
Thurgarton
Morton
Bleasby
Thorpe
Hawton
Barnby
Brinsley
Hucknall Torkard
Shirewood Lo.
Epperston
Gonaldston
Rolleston
Staythorpe
Balderton
Greasley
Woodborough
Lowdham
Hoveringham
Elston
Syerston
Cotham
Eastwood
Watnall Ha.
Lambley Ha.
Arnold
Knighton
Sibthorpe
Shelton
Bulwell Ho.
Red Hill Lo.
Burton Joyce
Flinham
Watnall
Bulwell
Daybrook
Lambley
Bulcote
Gunthorpe
E.st Bridgford
Hawksworth
Flawborough
Staunton
Allsworth
Basford
Carrington
Shelford
Gaw
Colston
Thornton
Orston
Kilvington
Cossal
Strelly
Bilborough
Sneinton
Gedling
Stoke Bardolph
Newton
Scarrington
Aslacton
Elton
Ripley
Radford
NOTTINGHAM
Saxondale
Bingham
Whatton
Trowell
Wollaton Hall
Colwick
Radcliff
Whatton
To Grantham
Stapleford
Lenton
Holme Pierrepont
Cropwell Butler
Tithby
Granby
Sutton
Bramcote
Beeston
Gamston
Grantham Ca.
Cropwell Bishop
Bronstone
To Grantham
Chillwell
Wilford
Edwalton
Cotgrave
Clipston
Owthorpe
Lungar
Attenboro
Clifton
Barton
To Ilkeston
Plumtree
Normanton
Colston Basset
Ruddington
Bradmore
Keyworth
Finrutton
From Derby R.ly To
Thrumpton
Bunny
Stanton on the Wolds
Gotham
W.m Leake
Kingston
Ratcliffe
Wysall
Hickling
Keyworth
Widmerpool
Broughton Sulney
Kegworth
Sutton
Cortlingstock
Willoughby
To Melton Mowbray
Bonington
Remnston
Stanford Ha.
Normanton
Stanford
Loughborough
NOTTINGHAMSHIRE.

NEWSTEAD ABBEY

Oxfordshire

A county of England, 47 miles in length, and 29 in breadth; bounded by Buckinghamshire, Gloucestershire, Berkshire, Warwickshire, and Northamptonshire. It is divided into 14 hundreds, which contain 1 city, 12 market towns, 280 parishes, and 51 villages. The air is sweet, mild, pleasant, and healthy, for which reason it contains several gentlemen's seats; and the soil, though various, is fertile in corn and grass, and the hills are shaded with woods. It is also a great sporting country, there being abundance of game preserved here. It has no manufactures of any account, being chiefly agricultural. Its chief city is Oxford. Population, 161,643. It sends 9 members to parliament.

Banbury

It is a large, well-built town, and its markets are well served with provisions. It is the second town for beauty in the county, and seated on the river Charwell. The houses are generally built with stone, and the church is a large, handsome structure. It has been long noted for its cakes and cheese, and is 78 miles from London. Market, Thursday. Population, 7366.

Blenheim House and Park

The demesne and mansion in the neighbourhood of Oxford and Woodstock, which were given to the Duke of Marlborough for his brilliant successes in the war against the French. It is named after Blenheim, a village lying on the Danube, near which the Duke and Prince Eugene, with the allied army, defeated the French and Bavarians, in August, 1704.

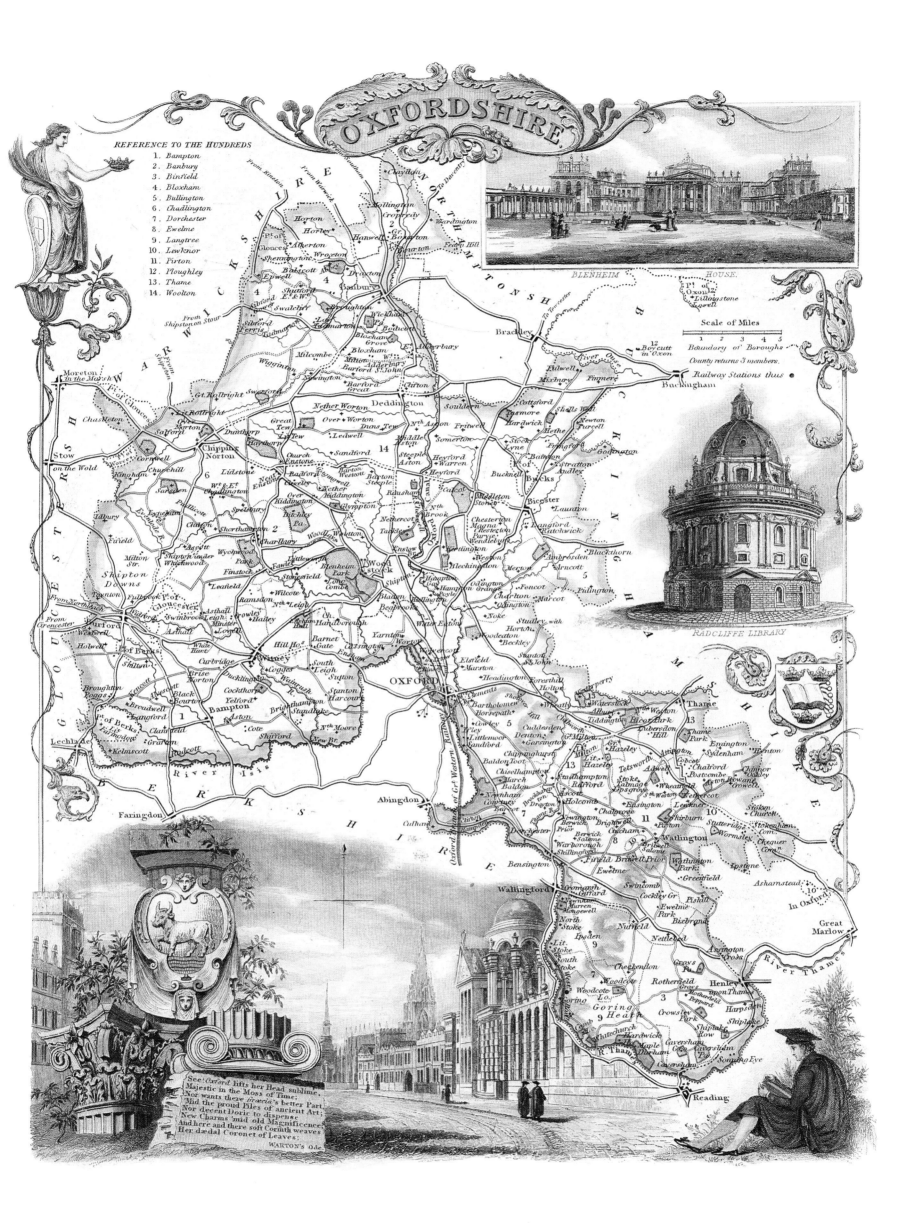

OXFORDSHIRE

REFERENCE TO THE HUNDREDS

1. Bampton
2. Banbury
3. Binfield
4. Bloxham
5. Bullington
6. Chadlington
7. Dorchester
8. Ewelme
9. Langtree
10. Lewknor
11. Pirton
12. Ploughley
13. Thame
14. Woolton

BLENHEIM HOUSE.

Scale of Miles
Boundary of Boroughs
County returns 3 members.
Railway Stations thus

RADCLIFFE LIBRARY

See Oxford lifts her Head sublime
Majestic in the Moss of Time.
Nor wants there Graecia's better Part,
Mid the proud Piles of ancient Art;
Nor decent Doric to dispense
New Charms 'mid old Magnificence;
And here and there soft Corinth weaves
Her dædal Coronet of Leaves;

WARTON's Ode.

Oxford

It is seated at the confluence of the Thames and Cherwell, on an eminence almost surrounded by meadows, except on the eastern side. The whole town, with the suburbs, is of a circular form, 3 miles in circumference. It consists chiefly of two spacious streets, which cross each other in the middle of the town. It is chiefly celebrated for its university, which is said to have been founded by Alfred, but is generally supposed to have been of even earlier origin. Here are 20 colleges, and 5 halls, several of which stand in the streets, and give the city an air of magnificence, which has obtained for it the name of the City of Cathedrals. The colleges are very wealthy, but are retained exclusively by the Established Church. The number of students is usually about 2000. Among the libraries in the university, the most distinguished is the Bodleian, founded by Thomas Bodley; those of All Souls' College, Christ Church, Queen's, New College, St. John's, Exeter, and Corpus Christi. Among other public buildings, are the Theatre, the Ashmolean Museum, the Clarendon Printing-house, the Radcliffe Infirmary, and a fine Observatory. It is 58 miles from London. Markets, Wednesday and Saturday. Population, 23,834.

CHRIST CHURCH

One of the colleges of Oxford university, founded by Cardinal Wolsey in 1524, and remodelled by Henry VIII. after the Cardinal's fall. It is a very noble institution, and is immediately connected with the bishopric of Oxford; its chapel being the cathedral church, and the dean and chapter having the sole management of all its affairs. It has a good library. Its buildings are on a very fine scale, and in the gate-way hangs the bell, famed as Great Tom of Oxford.

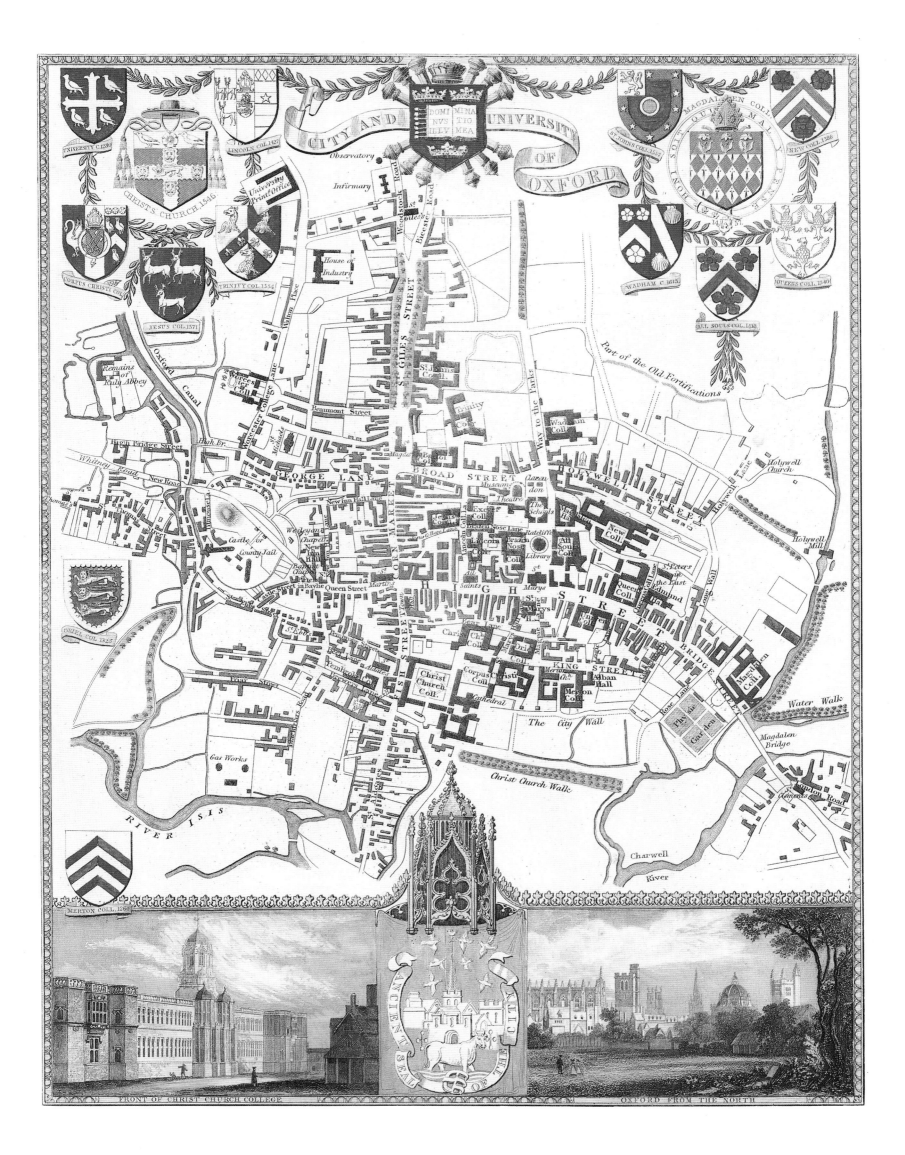

CITY AND UNIVERSITY OF OXFORD

DOMI NVS ILLV MINA TIO MEA

UNIVERSITY C.1280

LINCOLN COL.1427

CHRIST'S CHURCH 1546

University Print Office

CORPUS CHRISTI COLL

TRINITY COL 1554

JESUS COL 1571

ST JOHN'S COLL 1557

MAGDALEN COLL

HON SOIT QUI MAL Y PENSE

NEW COLL 1386

WADHAM C.1613

ALL SOULS COL 1413

QUEENS COLL 1340

ORIEL COL 1323

MERTON COLL 1264

Observatory

Infirmary

House of Industry

Walton Place

Beaumont Street

Woodstock Road

Bicester Road

ST GILES STREET

St Johns Coll.

Trinity Coll.

Way to the Parks

Part of the Old Fortifications

Remains of Rewly Abbey

Oxford Canal

Worcester Coll

St Michaels

Worcester College Lane

High Bridge Street

High Br.

Whitby Road

New Road

GEORGE LANE

Magdalen Hall

BROAD STREET

Museum

Theatre

Clarendon

The Schools

HOLYWELL STREET

Holywell Church

Holywell Lane

Holywell Mill

Thomas's

Rink

Castle or County Jail

Wesleyan Chapel

New Inn Hall

New Inn Hall Lane

Exeter Coll

Jesus Coll

St Johns Lane

Lincoln Coll.

Brazen Nose Lane

Rose Lane

Brazen Nose Coll

Ratcliffe Library

All Souls Coll

New Coll.

Long Wall

St Peters in the East

Edmund

Bocardo Charity

St Thomas

Queen Street

Castle Street in Baylie

HIGH STREET

St Martins

Town Hall

All Saints

St Marys

St Marys H.

Queens Coll.

Queen's College Lane

St Edmund Hall

BRIDGE STREET

Magdalen Coll

ST EBBS

Pembroke St

Abbots

Brewers Road

Carfax

Tom Gate

Corpus Christi Coll

Christ Church Coll.

Oriel Coll.

KING STREET

Merton Ch.

St Alban Hall

Merton Coll.

Rose Lane

Physic Garden

Water Walk

Magdalen Bridge

Christ Church Coll.

Cathedral

The City Wall

London Road

Cowley Road

Gas Works

Christ Church Walk

Charwell River

RIVER ISIS

ANCIENT SEAL OF THE CITY

FRONT OF CHRIST CHURCH COLLEGE

OXFORD FROM THE NORTH

Rutlandshire

The smallest county of England, 15 miles in length, and 11 in breadth. It is bounded by Leicestershire, Nottinghamshire, Lincolnshire, and Northamptonshire. It contains 48 parishes, and two market towns. It yields good stone for building purposes. The air is very good, and the soil rich, producing excellent corn, and feeding a great number of cattle and sheep. The principal rivers are the Welland and the Guash, or Wash. It is well wooded, and abounds in gentlemen's seat. Oakham, in the fertile vale of Catmose, is the county town. Population 21,302. It sends two members to parliament.

Oakham

It is pretty well built, and has a free-school and an hospital. It is the county town. It is seated in a rich valley, called the Vale of Catmos, and is 95 miles from London. Markets, Monday and Saturday. Population, 2726.

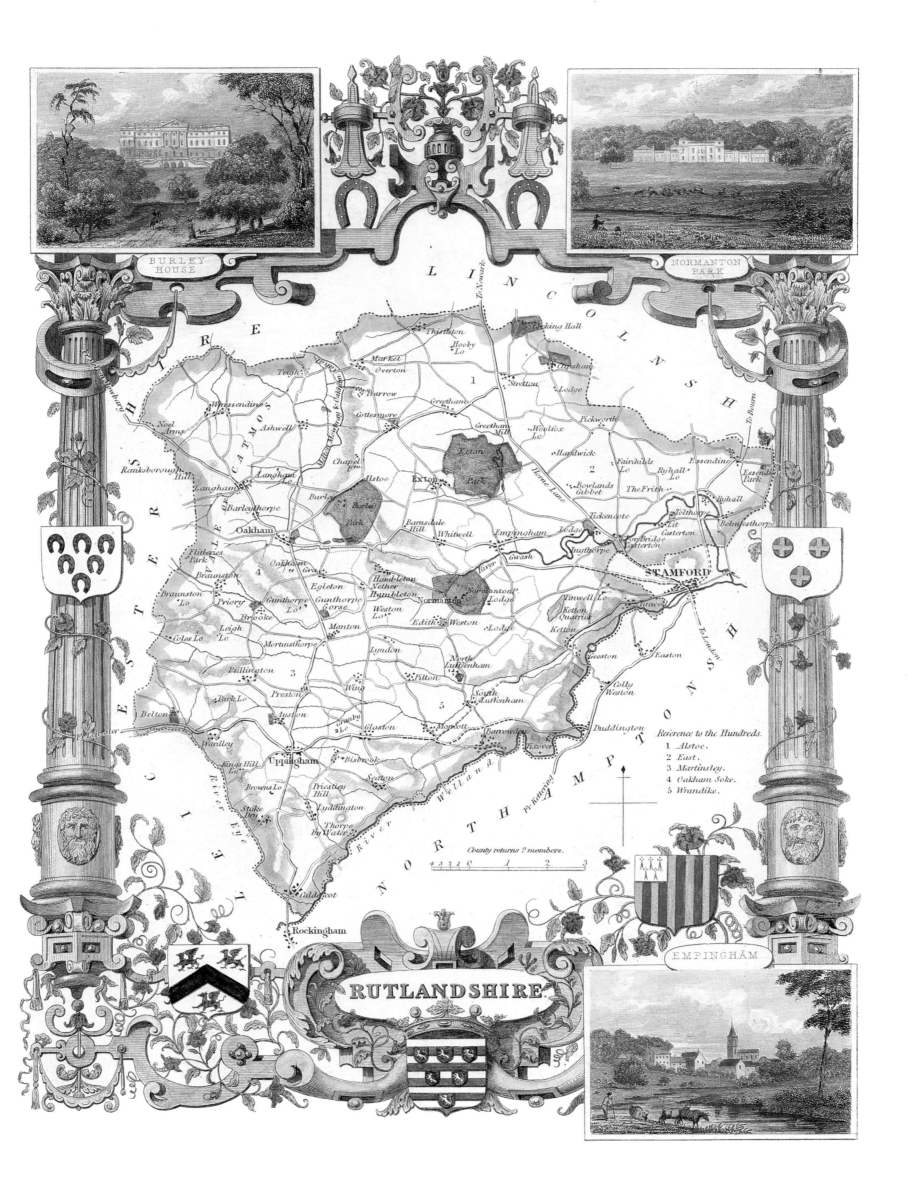

BURLEY
HOUSE

NORMANTON
PARK

LINCOLNSHIRE

To Newark
To Bourn
To London

Thistleton
Hooby Lo
Market Overton
Teigh
Barrow
Greetham
Stretton
Lodge
Cocking Hall
Gipsham
Pickworth
Woolfox Lo
Hardwick
Fairfields Lo
Ryhall Lo
Essendine
Essendine Park

Whissendine
Ashwell
Cottesmore
Greetham Mill
Ketton Park
Bowlands Gibbet
The Frith
Ryhall

Noel Arms
Chapel Em
Alstoe
Exton
Empingham
Lodge
Tolethorpe
Lit Casterton
Belmesthorpe

Ranksborough Hill
Langham
Langham Lo
Burley
Burley Park
Barnsdale Hill
Whitwell
Lodge
Inysthorpe
CoryBridge Casterton
Tickencote

Barleythorpe
Oakham
River Gwash
STAMFORD

Flitteris Park
Oakham Gra
Egleton
Hambleton Nether Hambleton
River Gwash
Tinwell Lo
Tinwell

Braunston
Braunston Lo
Priory
Gunthorpe Lo
Gunthorpe Gorse
Normanton
Normanton P. Lodge
Ketton Quarries
Ketton

Brooke
Leigh
Coles Lo
Manton
Weston Lo
Edith Weston
Lodge

Mortinsthorpe
Lyndon
North Luffenham
Geeston
Easton

Fillington
Pilton
Colly Weston

Park Lo
Preston
Wing
South Luffenham
Duddington

Belton
Ayston
Granby Lo
Glaston
Morcott
Barrowden
Duddington
By Kettering

Wardley
Thixover

King's Hill Lo
Uppingham
Bisbrook
Seaton

Browns Lo
Priestley Hill
Lyddington

Stoke Dry
Thorpe by Water

Caldecot
Rockingham

River Eye
River Welland
NORTHAMPTONSHIRE

Reference to the Hundreds.
1 Alstoe.
2 East.
3 Martinsley.
4 Oakham Soke.
5 Wrandike.

County returns 2 members.
4 3 2 1 0   1   2   3

RUTLANDSHIRE

EMPINGHAM

Shropshire

An English county, 44 miles in length, and 28 in breadth; bounded by Cheshire, Denbighshire, Montgomeryshire, Herefordshire, and Staffordshire. It contains 170 parishes, and 16 market towns. The principal rivers are, the Severn, which runs through the midst of the county, the Terne, the Clun, and the Rhea, with several other small streams. The west and south parts are mountainous, some points being nearly 2000 feet high, and several surpassing 1000; but the east and north more plain and level; however, the soil is pretty fertile everywhere, yielding corn and pastures, besides coal, iron, and other commodities. The air is sharp on the tops of the hills and mountains, but in the lower parts temperate enough. The great branches of manufacturing industry carried on here are all kinds of ironworks, woollens, and china, earthenware, &c. Shrewsbury is the capital. Population, 239,048. It sends 11 members to parliament.

SHREWSBURY

The capital of the county, so called from the Saxon word Scrobbesberig, which signifies a town built on a woody hill. It is well built, well lighted, and well paved, and is the chief mart for a coarse kind of woollen cloth made in Montgomeryshire, called Welsh webs, which are bought up in all parts of the country, and dressed here. Much of the Welsh flannel is also bought at Welshpool by the drapers of this place, which is indeed a common mart for all sorts of Welsh commodities. One great ornament of this town is the Quarry, one of the finest promenades in England. It is beautifully situated in a sort of horseshoe, formed by the river Severn, 154 miles from London. Markets, for corn, cattle, and provisions, Wednesday and Saturday; and Thursday, for Welsh cottons, friezes, and flannels. Fairs, Saturday after March 15, Wednesday after Easter week, Wednesday before Holy Thursday, July 3, August 12, October 2, and December 12. Population, 21,517.

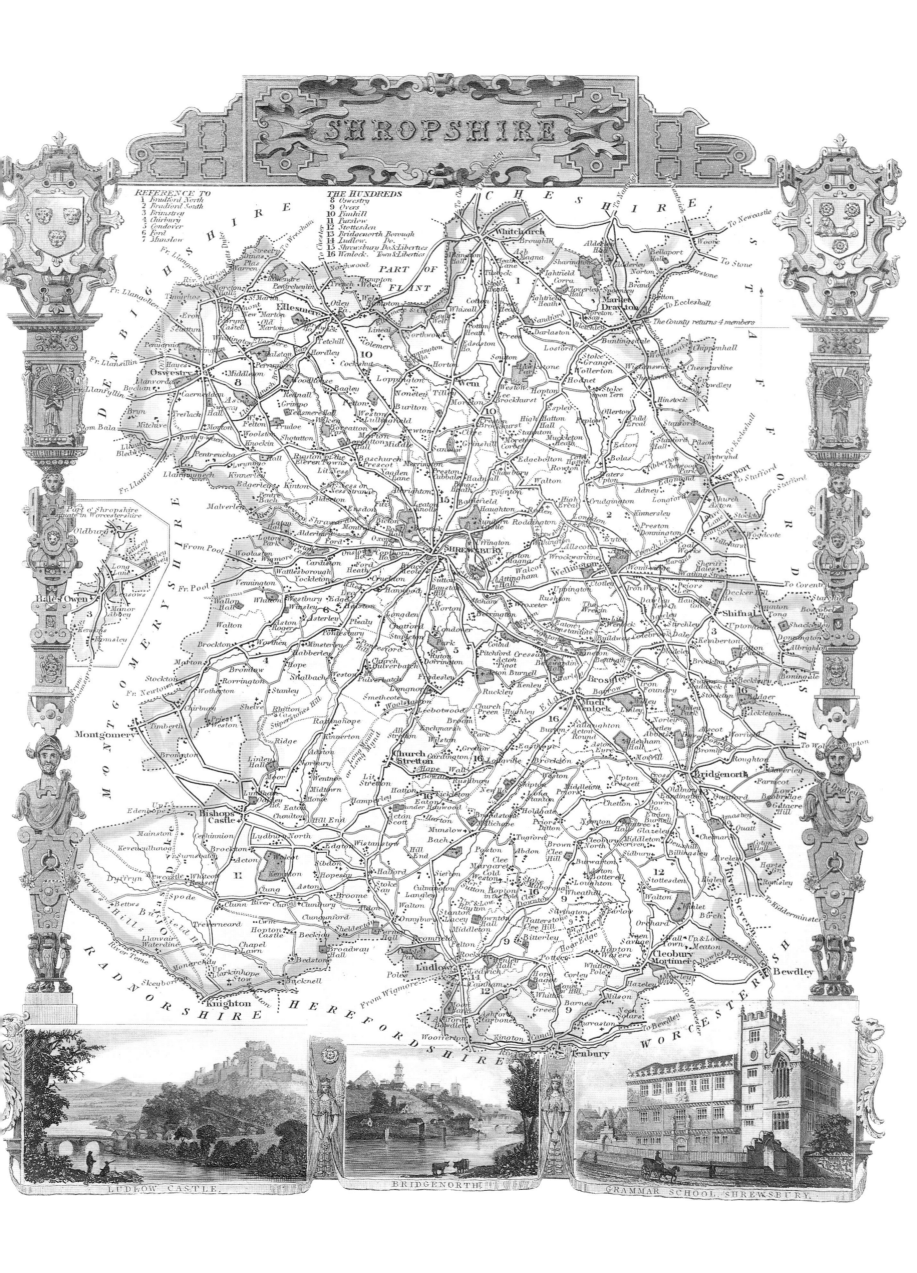

SHROPSHIRE

REFERENCE TO THE HUNDREDS
1 Bradford North
2 Bradford South
3 Brimstry
4 Chirbury
5 Condover
6 Ford
7 Munslow
8 Oswestry
9 Overs
10 Pimhill
11 Purslow
12 Stottesden
13 Bridgenorth Borough
14 Ludlow Do.
15 Shrewsbury Do. & Liberties
16 Wenlock

The County returns 4 members

LUDLOW CASTLE.

BRIDGENORTH.

GRAMMAR SCHOOL, SHREWSBURY.

Somersetshire

A county of England, lying on the Bristol Channel, and bounded by Gloucestershire, Wiltshire, Dorsetshire, and Devonshire. Its length is about 65 miles, and its breadth between 30 and 40. It is divided into 40 hundreds, which contain 3 cities, 33 market towns, and 482 parishes. The air, in the lower grounds, is universally mild, and generally wholesome. It is hilly, and the Mendip chain has heights of about 1000 feet. The principal rivers are the Parret, Ivel, Chew, Axe, Thone, Brent, Exe, Frome, and Avon. Coal, and various metals, with good building and other kinds of stone, are found here. Corn, &c. are raised here; but cattle, sheep, cheese, &c. are more abundantly produced. Manufactures of several kinds are carried on in its towns, and some places have a great trade. Taunton is the county town. Population, 435,982. It sends 13 members to parliament.

TAUNTON

It has long been the principal seat of the manufacture of coarse woollen goods, such as serges, corduroys, sagathies, druggets, shalloons, &c., though somewhat decayed of late years. It is seated on the river Thone, which is navigable hence to the Parret, and so to Bridgewater; 144 miles from London. Markets, Wednesday and Saturday. Population, 12,066.

GLASTONBURY

It principally consists of two streets. Its abbey was formerly the most magnificent in the world, the domains and revenue of which were immense. It was anciently called the Isle of Avalon, into which no person, not even a bishop or prince, was allowed to enter without leave from the abbot, to whom this power was granted by Canute the Dane. Extensive ruins of this immense range of buildings are still remaining. The principal manufacture here is stockings. Nearly adjoining, on a high steep hill, is placed the tower of a church, called the Tor, which lifts its head into the clouds, and is an object of admiration to travellers, and even serves as a landmark to seamen in the Bristol Channel. It is situated in a low, marshy country, nearly encompassed with rivers, 129 miles from London. Market, Tuesday. Population, 3314.

MENDIP HILLS

A range of hills in Somersetshire, being at its highest points about 1,000 feet above the sea. They consist of mountain limestone and old red sandstone chiefly, and abound in combes, or narrow chasms, and caverns, in which many singular fossils have been found. Coal, copper, lead, galena, zinc, &c. &c. are found in abundance. There is good pasturage for sheep and cattle on the sides of these hills.

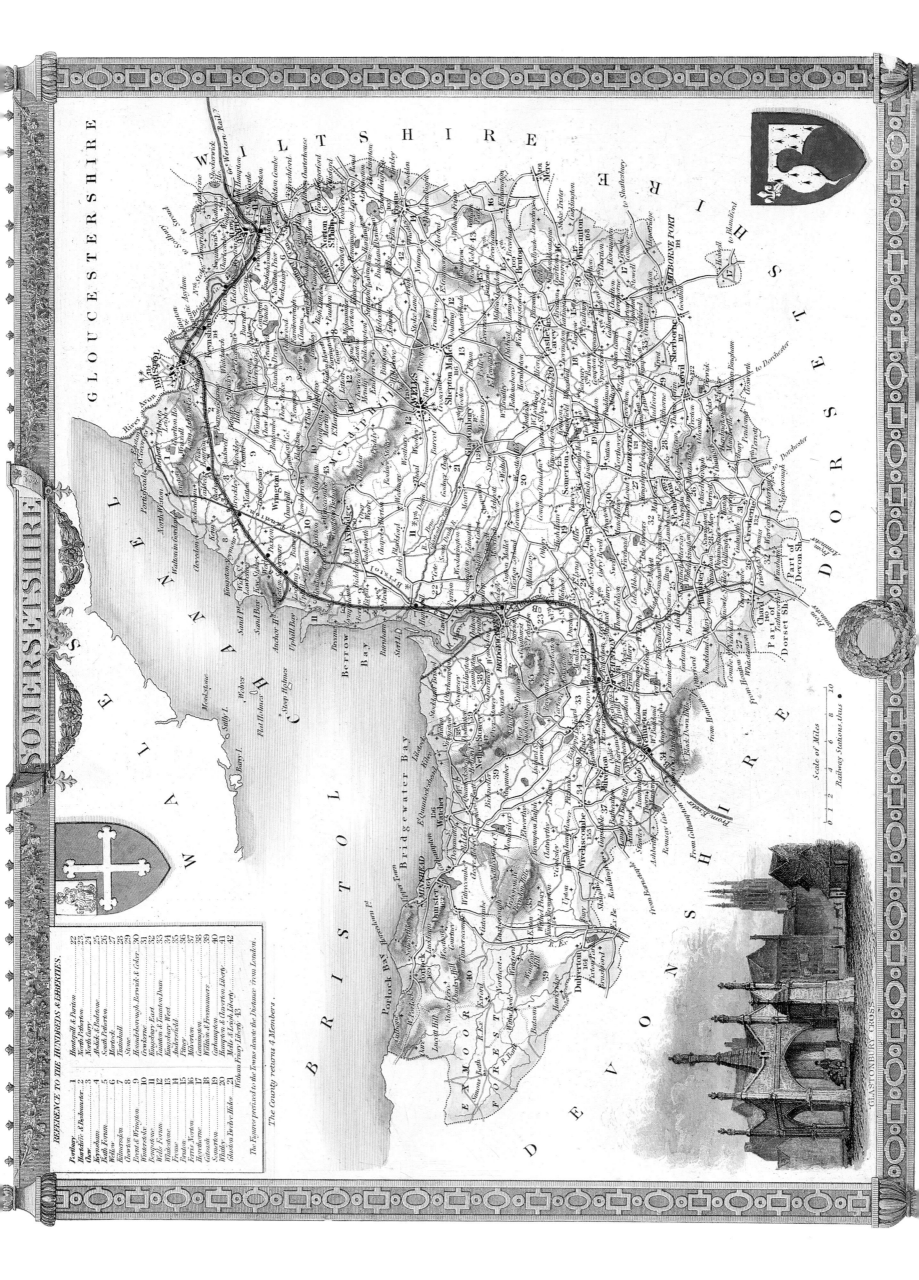

GLASTONBURY CROSS.

Scale of Miles

Railway Stations, thus •

Bath

This city, which is beautifully situated on the river Avon, has been famous from the times of the Romans for its hot springs; but it has not lately been so much resorted to, owing to the more recent celebrity of other springs in this country, and on the continent. It is built almost entirely of stone, and laid out in squares, crescents, terraces, &c., which rise above each other, from the Avon to the summit of the hill. The abbey church, the general hospital, and the dispensary, are fine buildings. Considerable manufactures of cloth and paper are carried on near Bath. It is 107 miles from London. Market, Saturday. Population, 38,304.

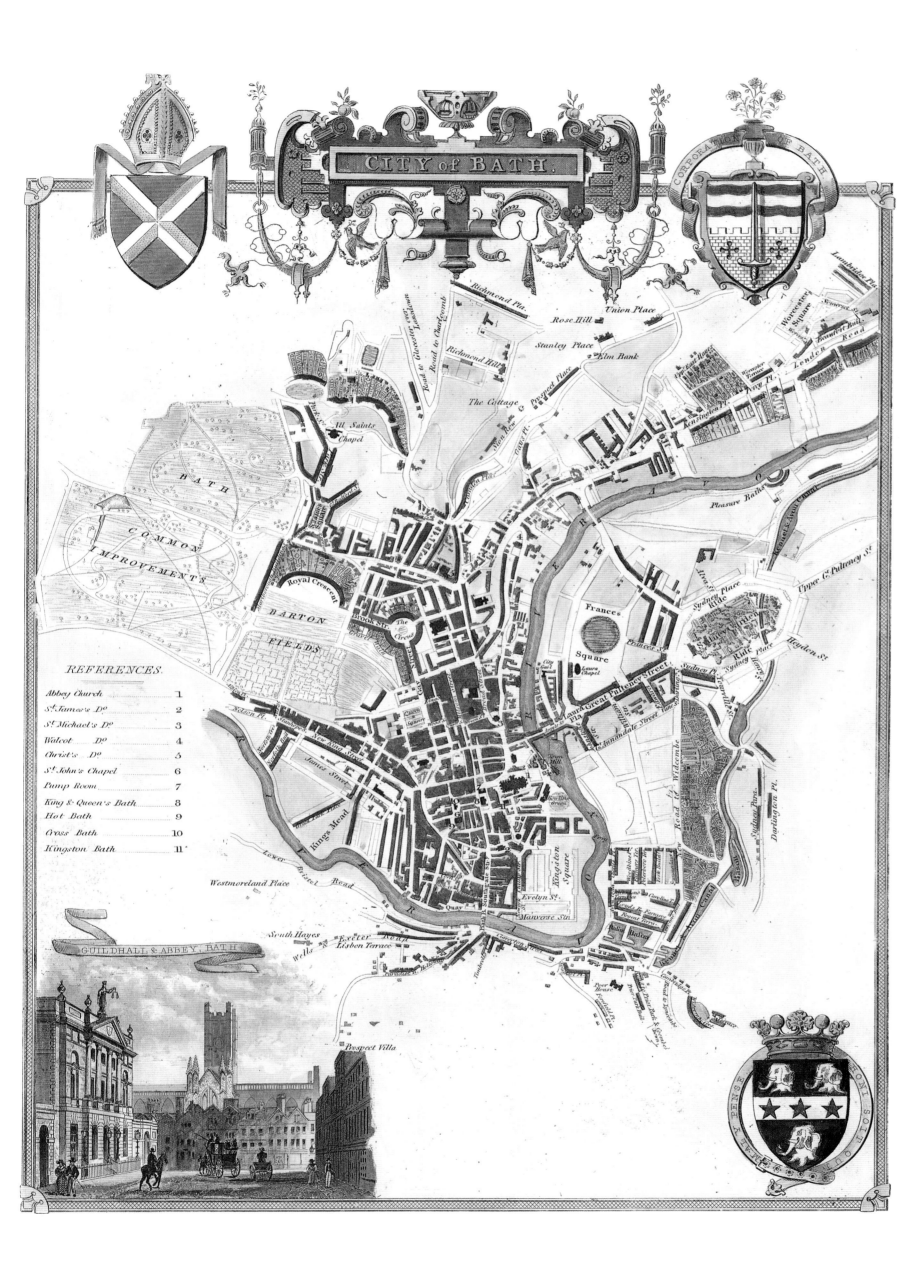

CITY of BATH.

REFERENCES.

Abbey Church	1
St James's Do	2
St Michael's Do	3
Walcot Do	4
Christ's Do	5
St John's Chapel	6
Pump Room	7
King & Queen's Bath	8
Hot Bath	9
Cross Bath	10
Kingston Bath	11

GUILDHALL & ABBEY, BATH.

Bristol

This sea-port stands at the confluence of the Avon and the Frome, about 9 miles from where the Avon discharges itself into the Bristol Channel. It occupies a noble position, rising range above range of houses to the top of a hill; but the old part is narrow and ill built, whilst the new parts are magnificent, the houses being made of stone, and much in the same style as Bath. The docks and harbours are extensive, as are the quays, to which the largest ships have access. The public buildings are numerous; amongst the finest of them may be mentioned the churches, the exchange, the railway buildings, the scientific and literary institutions, &c.. Bristol manufactures sugar, glass, floor-cloth, brass, iron, &c. &c.. It imports goods from all quarters of the world, but from Ireland most abundantly. But the trade has not lately been so great as it was. There are several colleges and high schools in this town. The neighbourhood is most beautiful and healthy, abounding in objects of curiosity, especially to the botanist and geologist. It is 110 miles from London. Markets, Wednesday, Friday, and Saturday. Population, 140,158.

Avon

A British word meaning river, which is the name of several in England, the largest of which springs near Naseby, in Northamptonshire, and falls, after a gently winding course of about 100 miles, into the Severn.

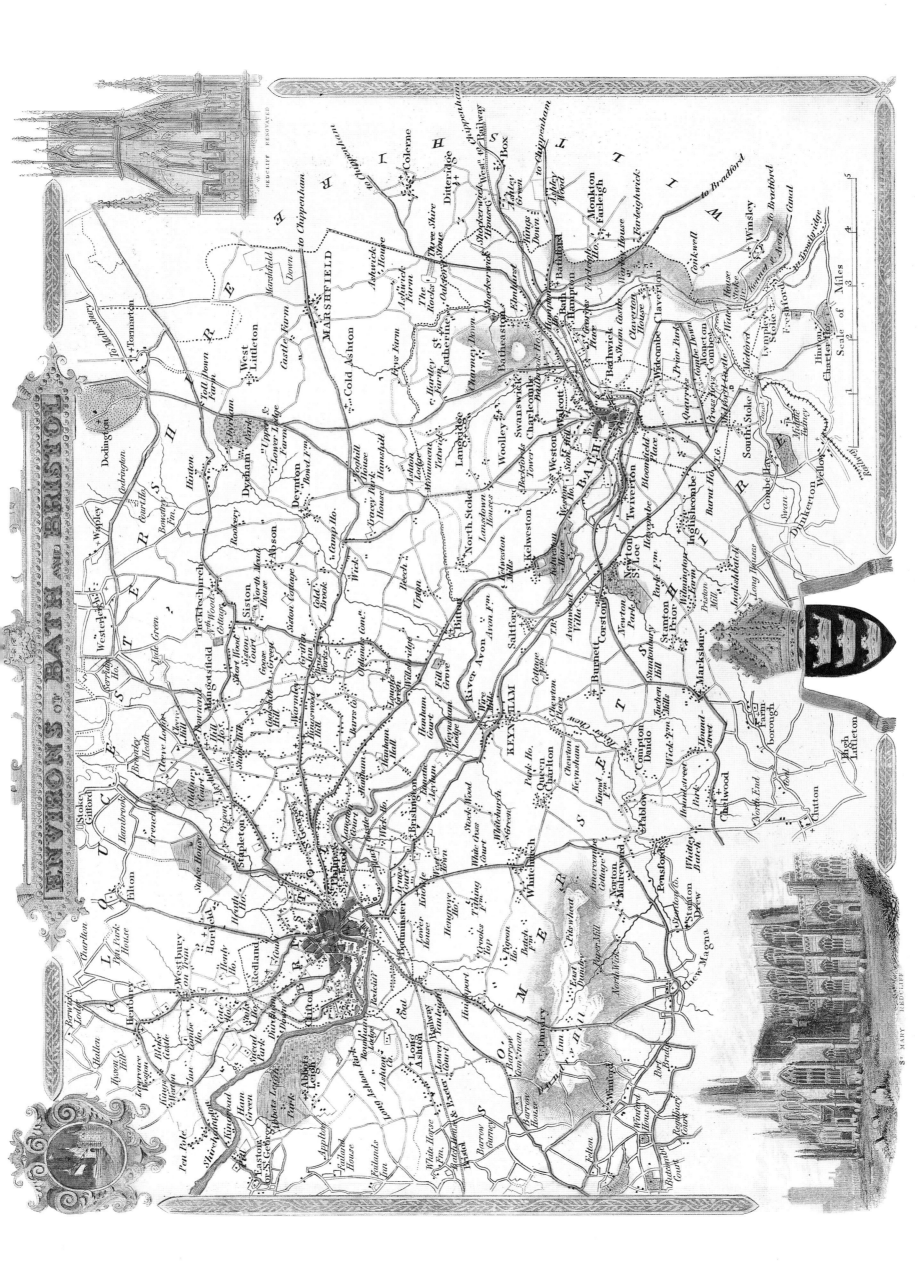

Staffordshire

A county of England, bounded by Shropshire, Cheshire, Derbyshire, Warwickshire, and Worcestershire. It is in length about 54 miles, and varies in breadth from 18 to 36. It is divided into 5 hundreds, which contain 1 city, 21 towns, 181 parishes, and 670 villages. The principal rivers are the Trent, Dove, Sow, Churnet, Stour, Penk, and Manifold. The air is reckoned pleasant, mild, and wholesome. The middle and southern parts are level and plain, and the soil is good and rich; the north is hilly, and full of heaths and moors. Staffordshire is famous for its potteries, its inland navigations, and its founderies, blast furnaces, slitting mills, and various other branches of the iron trade. The mines of coals, copper, lead, and iron ore are rich and extensive; and there are also numerous quarries of stone, alabaster, and limestone. Stafford is the county town. Population 510,504. It sends 17 members to parliament.

STAFFORD

It has a free-school, and a fine square market-place, in which is a handsome county-hall, and under it the market-house. The streets are large, and many of the houses are handsomely built. It has manufactures of cloth and shoes. It is situated in a plain on the river Sow, near a navigable canal, 135 miles from London. Market, Saturday. Population, 10,370.

TRENT

A large river in England, which rises in Staffordshire, issuing from three several springs between Congleton and Leek. Flowing through Staffordshire, it enters Derbyshire, crosses the southern angle of that county, and forms for a short space its separation from the counties of Lincoln and Nottingham; it then enters the latter county, and crossing it forms the boundary between that county and Lincolnshire, a corner of which it crosses, and then falls into the Humber below Gainsborough, after a course of about 200 miles, during which it receives the waters of several large streams. It is a large navigable river through the whole of Nottinghamshire, but has the inconvenience of being subject to great and frequent floods.

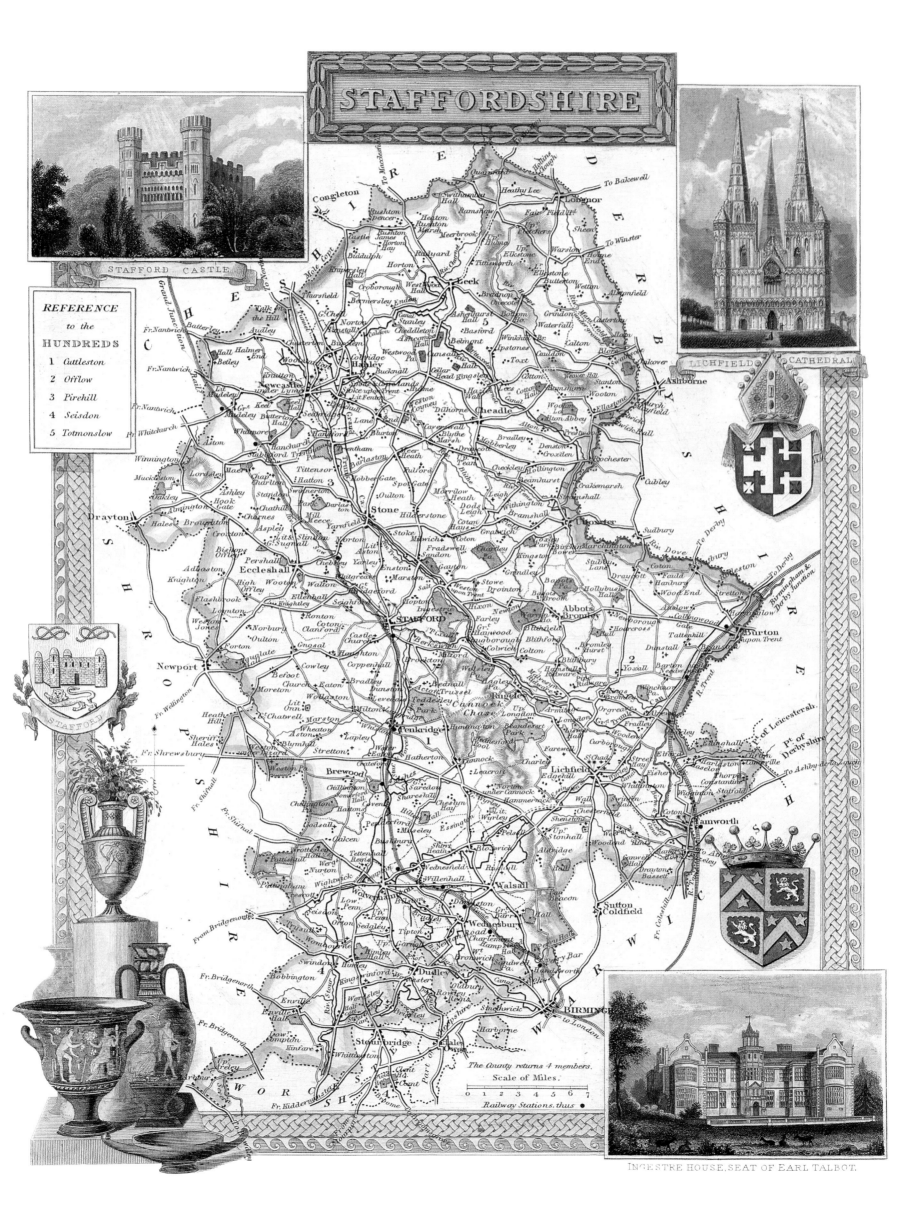

STAFFORDSHIRE

STAFFORD CASTLE

LICHFIELD CATHEDRAL

STAFFORD

The County returns 4 members.

Scale of Miles.

0 1 2 3 4 5 6 7

Railway Stations thus

INGESTRE HOUSE, SEAT OF EARL TALBOT.

Suffolk

A county of England, lying on the German Ocean, and bounded by Cambridgeshire, Norfolk, and Essex. It is nearly 50 miles long, and about 30 broad. It contains 575 parishes, and 28 market towns. The air is generally wholesome, but the soil is various; on the sea-coast it is sandy, and there are several small hills, which yield hemp, pease, and rye. The inland parts are clayey, and more full of trees. The borders towards Essex are fit for pastures, and the north west produce corn of all sorts. There are manufactures of broad-cloth, stuffs, and coarse linen, but not to any extent now. The principal rivers are, the Little Ouse, the Waveney, the Stour, the Breton, the Orwell or Gippe, the Deben, the Ore, and the Blyth. Ipswich and Bury St. Edmunds are the principal towns. Population, 315,073. It sends 11 members to parliament.

Bury St. Edmund's

It owes its name to a celebrated abbey, one of the largest and richest in the kingdom, founded in honour of Edmund, king of the East Angles, who was slain by the Danes and buried here. It has two fine churches, and is situated in a healthy, delightful spot, affording beautiful prospects. It is 72 miles from London. Markets, Wednesday and Saturday. Population, 12,538.

Ipswich

It is an ancient but irregularly built town, seated on the river Orwell, forming a sort of half-moon, or crescent, on its bank. Across the river there is a bridge leading to Stoke Hamlet. Here are several public buildings and a custom-house, with a good quay, and docks. Its present commerce depends upon the malting and exportation of corn to London, and timber to the different dockyards. It has a considerable coasting trade, and a small share of foreign commerce, but vessels of great burden are obliged to stop at some distance below the town. It is 69 miles from London. Markets, Tuesday and Thursday for small meat, Wednesday and Friday for fish, and Saturday for provisions of all kinds. Population, 24,940.

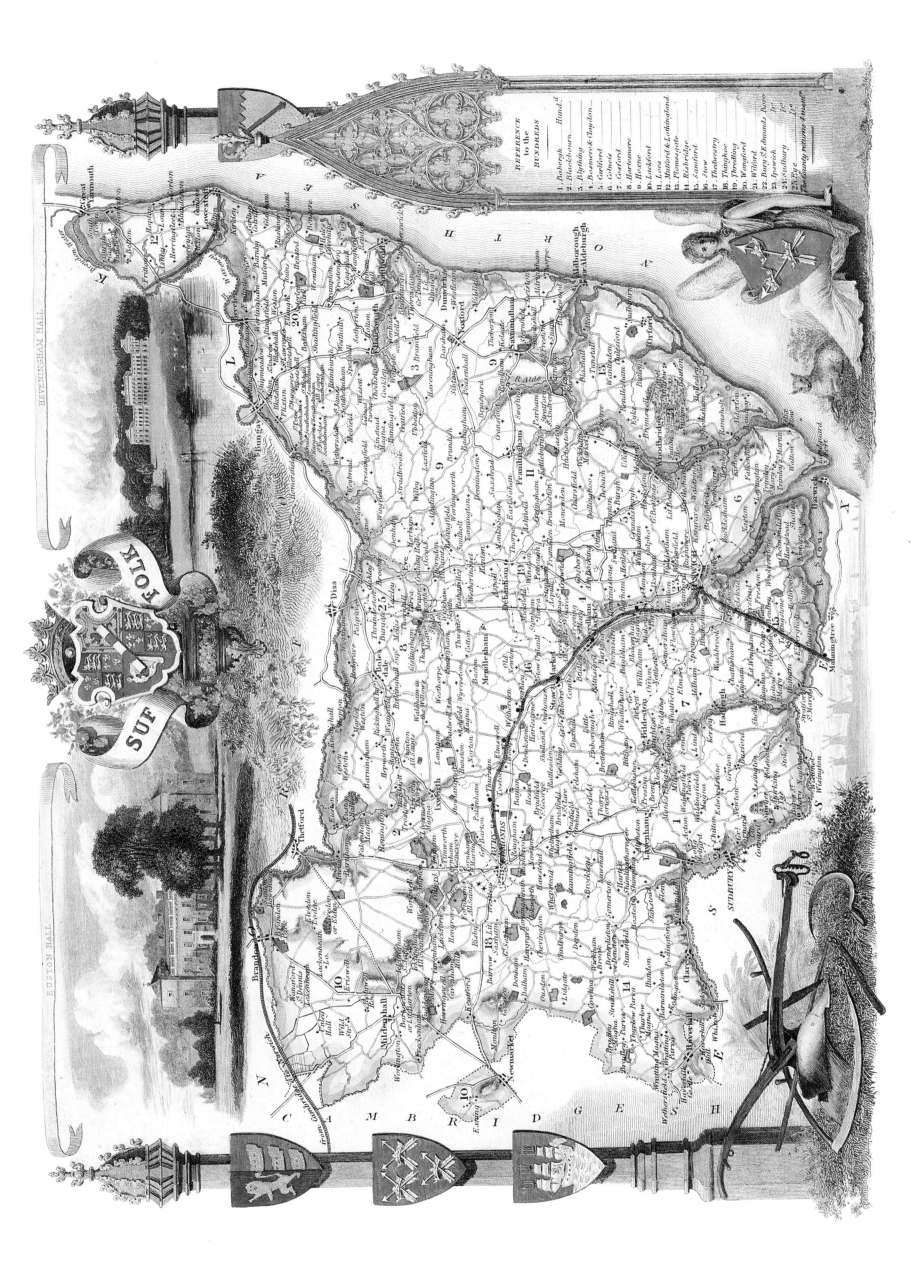

REFERENCE
to the
HUNDREDS

Hund.ᵈ

1. Babergh
2. Blackbourn
3. Blything
4. Bosmere & Claydon
5. Carlford
6. Colneis
7. Cosford
8. Hartesmere
9. Hoxne
10. Lackford
11. Loes
12. Mutford & Lothingland
13. Plomesgate
14. Risbridge
15. Samford
16. Stow
17. Thedwestry
18. Thingoe
19. Thredling
20. Wangford
21. Wilford
22. Bury St. Edmunds Boro.
23. Ipswich
24. Sudbury
25. Eye

Surrey

A county of England, bounded by Middlesex, Buckinghamshire, Kent, Sussex, Hampshire, and Berkshire. Its greatest length is about 39 miles, and its breadth 26. It is divided into 13 hundreds, which contain 11 market towns (including Southwark,) 140 parishes, and 650 villages and hamlets. It is crossed by the chalk hills, which are from 400 to 900 feet high; and the rest of the surface is low and fertile. The Thames, the Mole, the Wey, &c. water it. It produces all sorts of agricultural produce; and the wolds feed sheep, rabbits, &c. &c.. As part of the metropolis is included in it, it may be said to have manufactories also, and trade. Guildford, Croydon, and Kingston are its chief places. Population, 582,678. It sends 11 representatives to parliament.

CROYDON

The manor of Croydon has belonged, ever since the Conquest, to the archbishops of Canterbury, who had a venerable palace here, now, or lately, employed for a cotton manufactory. The new palace is at a little distance from the town. It has a very noble church. It is situated near the source of the Wandel. Its second fair is much frequented by persons from London, for walnuts. Market, Saturday. Population, 16,712. There is another small place of this name in Cambridgeshire. Population 441.

KINGSTON UPON THAMES

It is so called from its having been the residence of several of our Saxon kings, some of whom were crowned here, on a stage in the market-place. It is seated on the Thames, over which it has a wooden bridge of 22 piers and 20 arches. It is 10 miles from London. Market, Saturday. Population, 9760.

GUILDFORD

It is seated on the declivity of a hill, on the river Wey, which is navigable to the Thames, and by which a great quantity of timber is carried to London, not only from the neighbourhood, but from Sussex and Hampshire woods. It is 30 miles from London. Market, (chiefly for corn,) Saturday. Population, 4074.

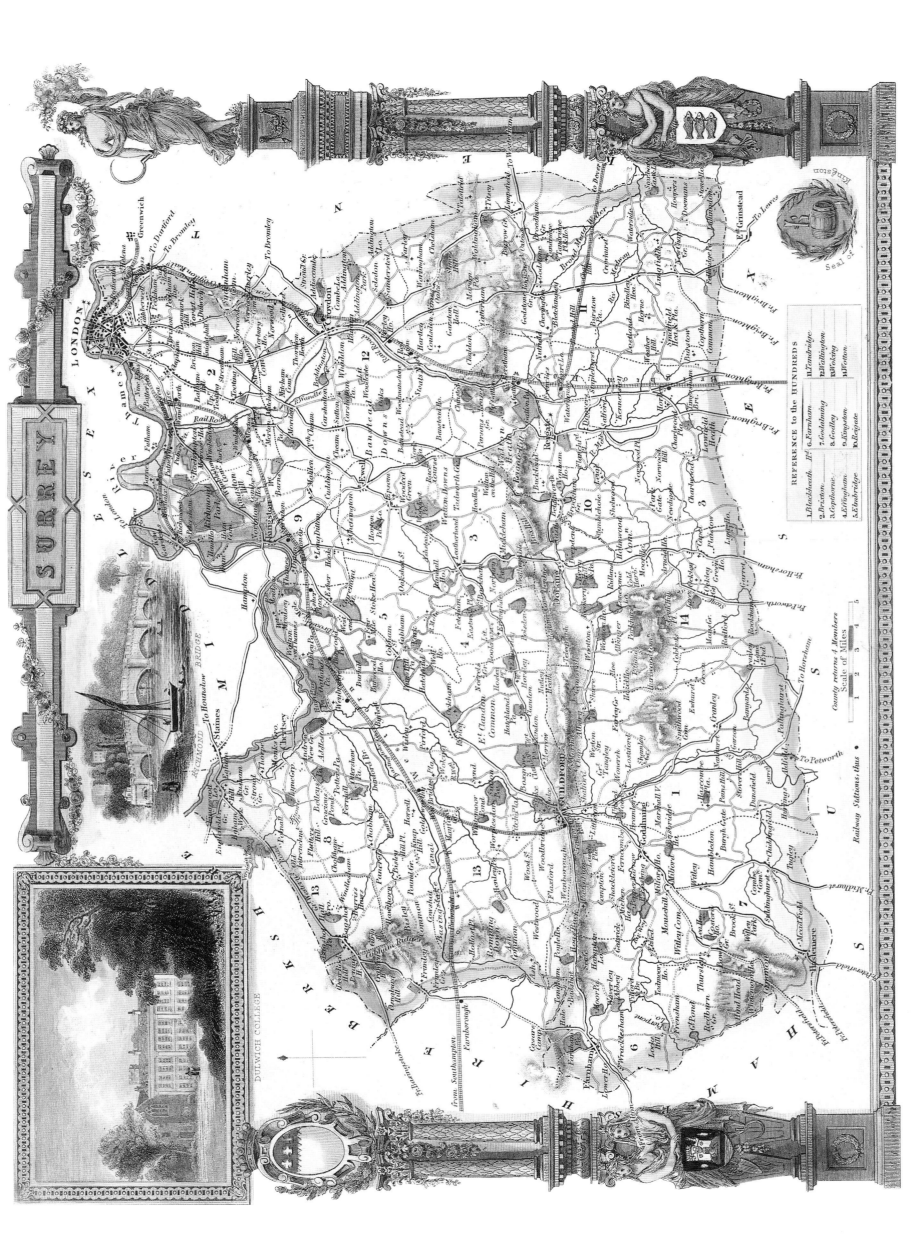

SURREY

LONDON

Sussex

An English county, 76 miles in length, and 20 in breadth; lying on the British Channel, and bounded by Hampshire, Surrey, and Kent. It contains 312 parishes, and 17 market towns. It is hilly, being crossed by the south line of chalk wolds; and is watered by the Arun, the Rother, and other streams. It yields good building-stone, and produces all kinds of agricultural produce. There are fine sheep-walks on the hills, and game is abundant. It has few manufactures, and not much trade. Its chief city is Chichester. Population, 299,753. It sends 18 members to parliament.

CHICHESTER

It is a neat and handsome city, seated in a plain, by the river Havant, by which it is encompassed on every side except the north. The market-place is in the centre of the town, from which the four principal streets are directed to the cardinal points of the compass, and bear the names of East, West, North and South Street. Its market is well supplied with provisions; it exports corn, malt, &c., has some foreign commerce, a manufactory of needles, and of baize, blankets, and coarse cloths. The haven, formed by a canal, cut from the city down into the bay, affords excellent lobsters. It is 61 miles from London. Markets, Wednesday, Friday, and Saturday. Population, 8512.

BRIGHTON

Or Brighthelmstone. This large town is beautifully situated on the south coast of England, and is a place of great resort in the bathing season, and during the latter part of autumn. It is of very recent growth, having been little beyond a fishing village till it was selected as a marine residence by George IV. It is a finely built place, especially towards the sea; and the royal palace, called the Pavilion, attracts attention by its grotesque style. It has a very fine chain pier, which is used as a promenade and landing-place. It is about 50 miles from London. Markets, Tuesday, Thursday and Saturday. Population, 46,661.

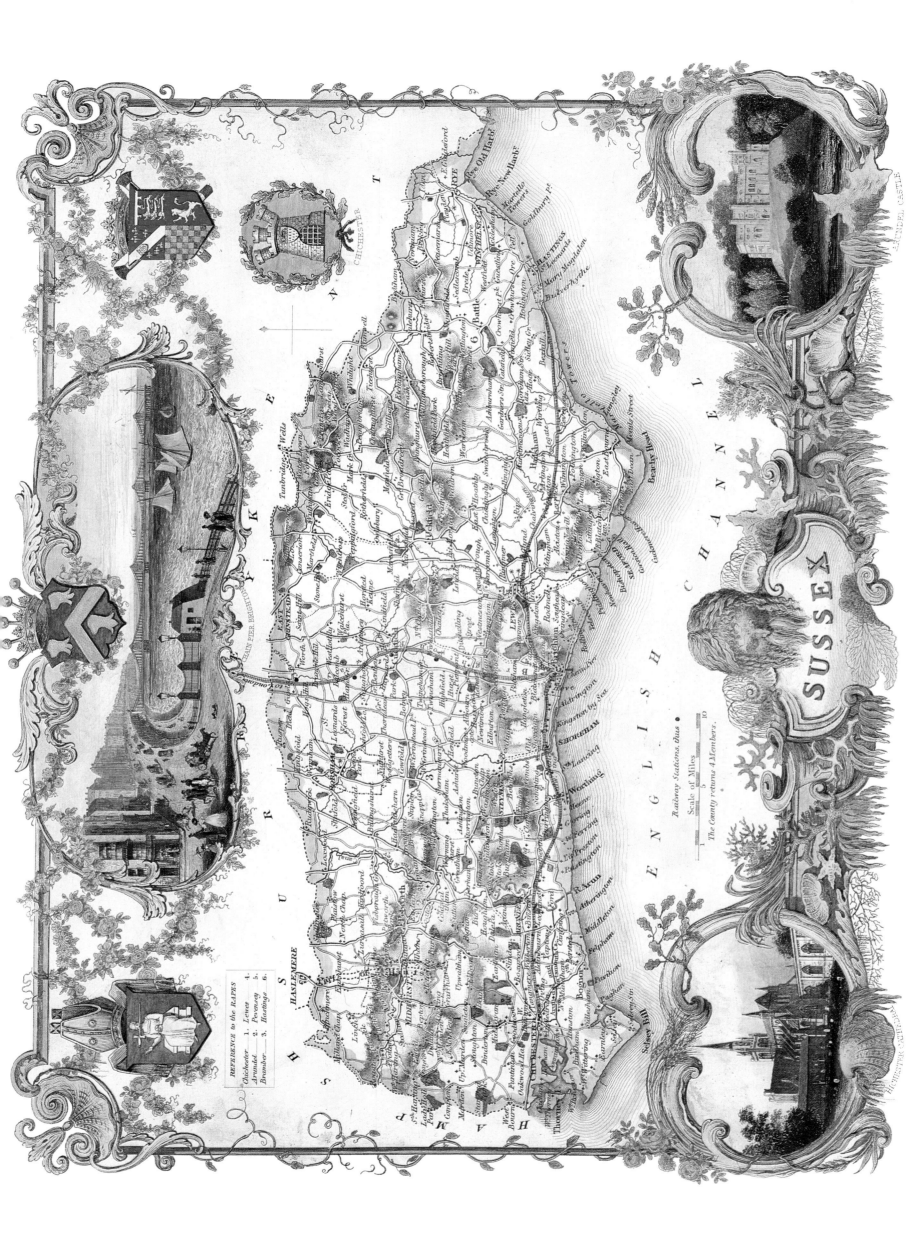

SUSSEX

ARUNDEL CASTLE

CHICHESTER

SUSSEX

KENT

SURREY

HAMP·SHIRE

HASLEMERE

ENGLISH CHANNEL

REFERENCE to the RAPES
Chichester   1.   Lewes   4.
Arundel   2.   Pevensey   5.
Bramber   3.   Hastings   6.

Railway Stations, thus   •
Scale of Miles
The County returns 4 Members.

Thanet

An island of the county of Kent, surrounded by the sea, except on the north east side, where it is bounded by the branches of the river Stour, now inconsiderable to what they were formerly. It contains several villages, and the sea-port towns of Margate and Ramsgate. Population, 31,466.

MARGATE

It stands on the north side of the isle of Thanet, within a small bay in the breach of the cliff. It is a place of great resort for sea-bathing, the shore being level and covered with fine sand, well adapted for that purpose. Great quantities of corn are exported hence, and vessels are frequently passing to and from the coast of Flanders. It is built on an easy ascent, the principal street being near a mile in length. It is 72 miles from London. Population, 11,050.

RAMSGATE

It is a sea-port of the Isle of Thanet, where two very substantial stone piers have been built for the security of the harbour, which is now capable of receiving 200 sail of ships. Ramsgate has some trade; but is much better known as a bathing-place. It is 72 miles from London. Markets, Wednesday and Saturday. Population, 10,909.

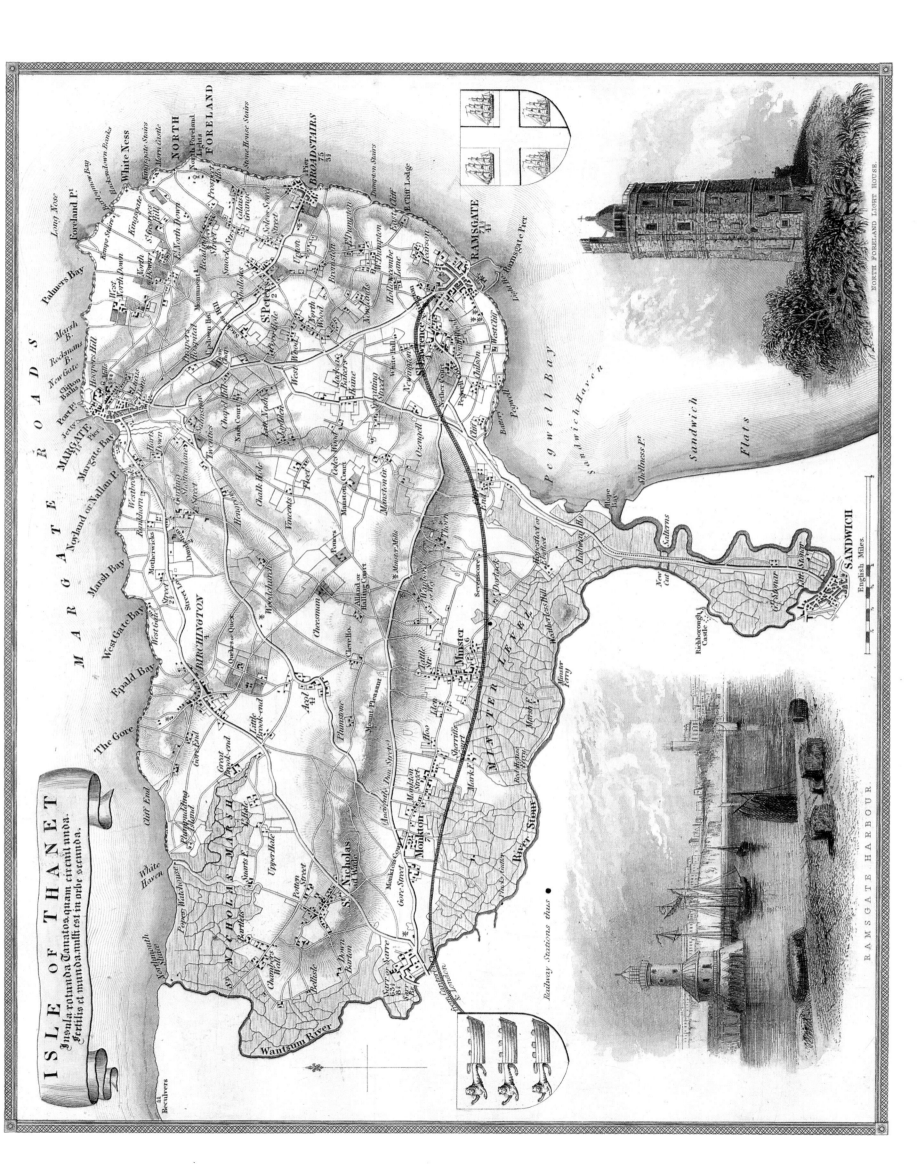

Warwickshire

An English county, 50 miles in length, and 35 in breadth; bounded by Worcestershire, Oxfordshire, Gloucestershire, Northamptonshire, Leicestershire, and Staffordshire. It contains 158 parishes, and 17 market towns. The air is mild and healthful, and the soil fertile, producing corn and pastures, particularly in the southern part, called the Vale of Red Horse. It has few hills; and is watered by the Avon, the Trent, and their feeders. Coal, iron, lime and building stone, &c. are abundant. It has some manufactures, and a good trade. Warwick is the chief town. Population, 401,715. It sends 10 members to parliament.

WARWICK

It is seated on a rock near the river Avon, and was fortified with a wall which is now in ruins, but it has still a strong and stately castle. It contains two parish churches, and in that of St. Mary's are several handsome tombs. The houses are well built, and the town principally consists of one regular built street, at each end of which is an ancient gate. It is adorned with a good free-school and a market house. It enjoys a good trade, and is 91 miles from London. Market, Saturday. Population, 9775.

BIRMINGHAM

This is one of the largest of our manufacturing towns; it is finely and healthily situated on the slope of a hill, with a few small streams near it, which afterwards flow either to the North Sea, or by the Severn to the Atlantic. The coal and iron district terminates some miles from the town, and the strata in its vicinity are only sands, gravels, and clays, whence the soil is very poor. The wealth of the town consists in its varied manufactures, which consist of all kinds of steel and iron goods from those made by the great rolling-mills, to the most exquisitely finished ornaments, and steel pens, glass, silver goods, papier-maché articles, &c. There are several churches, built in a good style of architecture, and the newer parts of the town also are well built; the railway termini and some of the manufactories are fine erections. King Edward's school has been rebuilt in a most elegant Gothic style, and the town-hall (which contains one of the noblest organs in Europe) is a grand building, constructed after the model of a Roman temple, and placed in a most commanding situation. Market, Thursday. Population, 182,922.

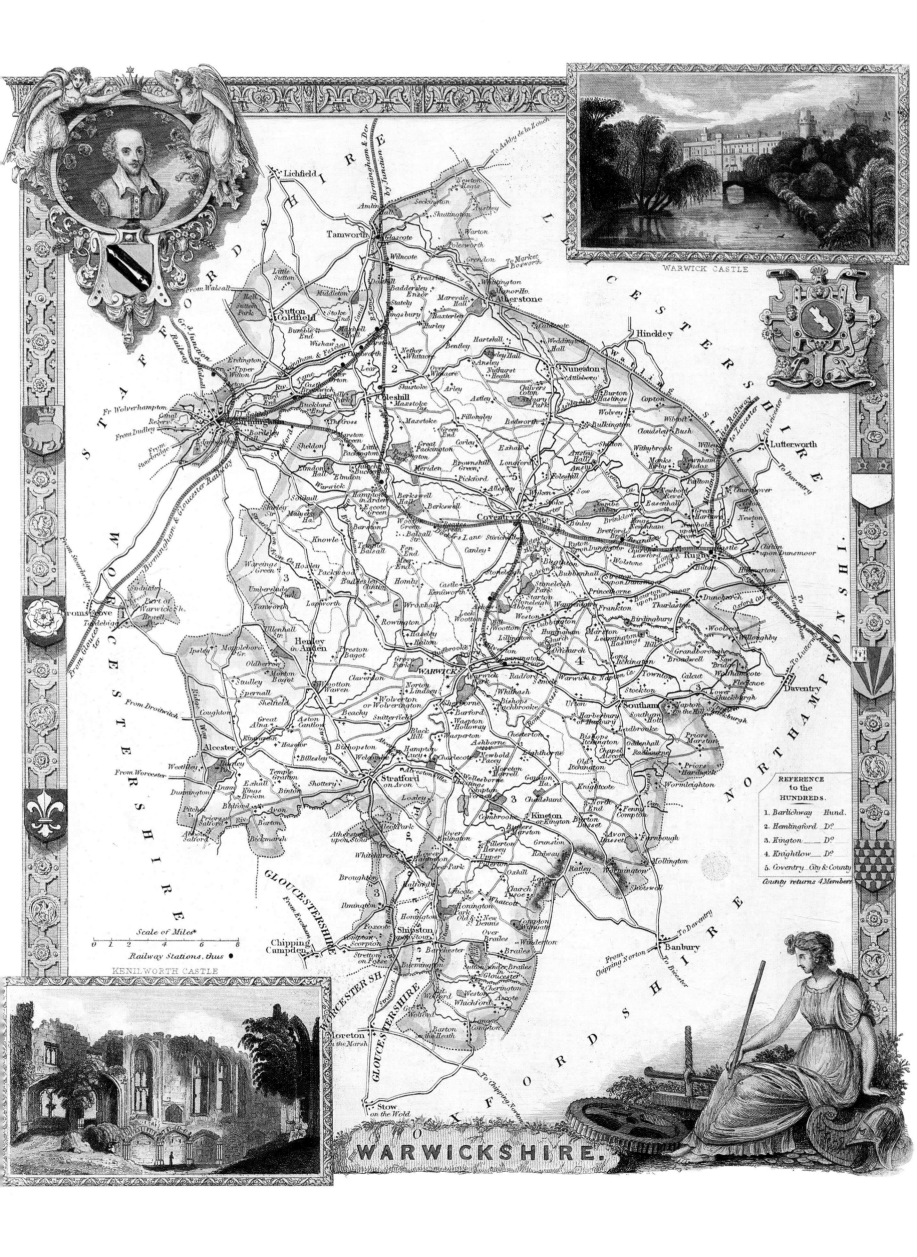

WARWICK CASTLE

KENILWORTH CASTLE

REFERENCE
to the
HUNDREDS.

1. Barlichway Hund.
2. Hemlingford Do.
3. Kington Do.
4. Knightlow Do.
5. Coventry City & County

County returns 4 Members

Scale of Miles
0 1 2 4 6 8

Railway Stations, thus ●

WARWICKSHIRE.

Westmoreland

An English county, 40 miles in length, and 21 in breadth, bounded by Cumberland, Lancashire, and Yorkshire. It contains 26 parishes and 8 market towns. The air is very sharp and cold, but healthy. It is a mountainous country; two ridges across the county, with peaks about 3000 feet high, and run towards the sea to the south west, where a bay of it washes this county. There are some valleys fruitful in corn and pastures, and the hills serve to feed a great number of sheep. The principal rivers are the Eden, the Ken, the Loan, the Eamon, the Tees, the Lowther, the Hunna, the Winster, the Lavennet-beck, and the Blinkern-beck. There also four noted lakes, called Ulles-water, Broad-water, Horns-water, and Winander-water. It yields coal, slate, building-stone of all kinds, and other valuable minerals. The principal town is Appleby, but Kendal is the most considerable for size, trade, and population. Population, 56,454. It sends 3 members to parliament.

APPLEBY

Almost surrounded by the river Eden. Formerly a Roman station. There is a castle here, the dungeon of which is very ancient. It is the county town, and 266 miles from London. Market, Saturday. Population, 2519.

KENDAL

Also called Kirby Candale, (that is, a church in a valley). It is the largest town in the county, and has been long noted for its woollen manufactories; particularly knit stockings, a thick stuff, called cottons, for the clothing of the people in the West Indies, and for sailors' jackets, and linsey-woolsey. There is likewise a considerable tannery; and fish-hooks, waste silk, and wool cards, are manufactured here. The mills for scouring, fulling, and friezing cloth, and for cutting and rasping dyeing-wood, &c. are well worth seeing. Kendal is pleasantly situated in a valley, among hills, upon the river Kent, or Kant, over which it has two stone bridges, and one of wood, with a harbour for boats, and communicating by a canal with all the late inland navigations. It is 259 miles from London. Market, Saturday. Population, 10,225.

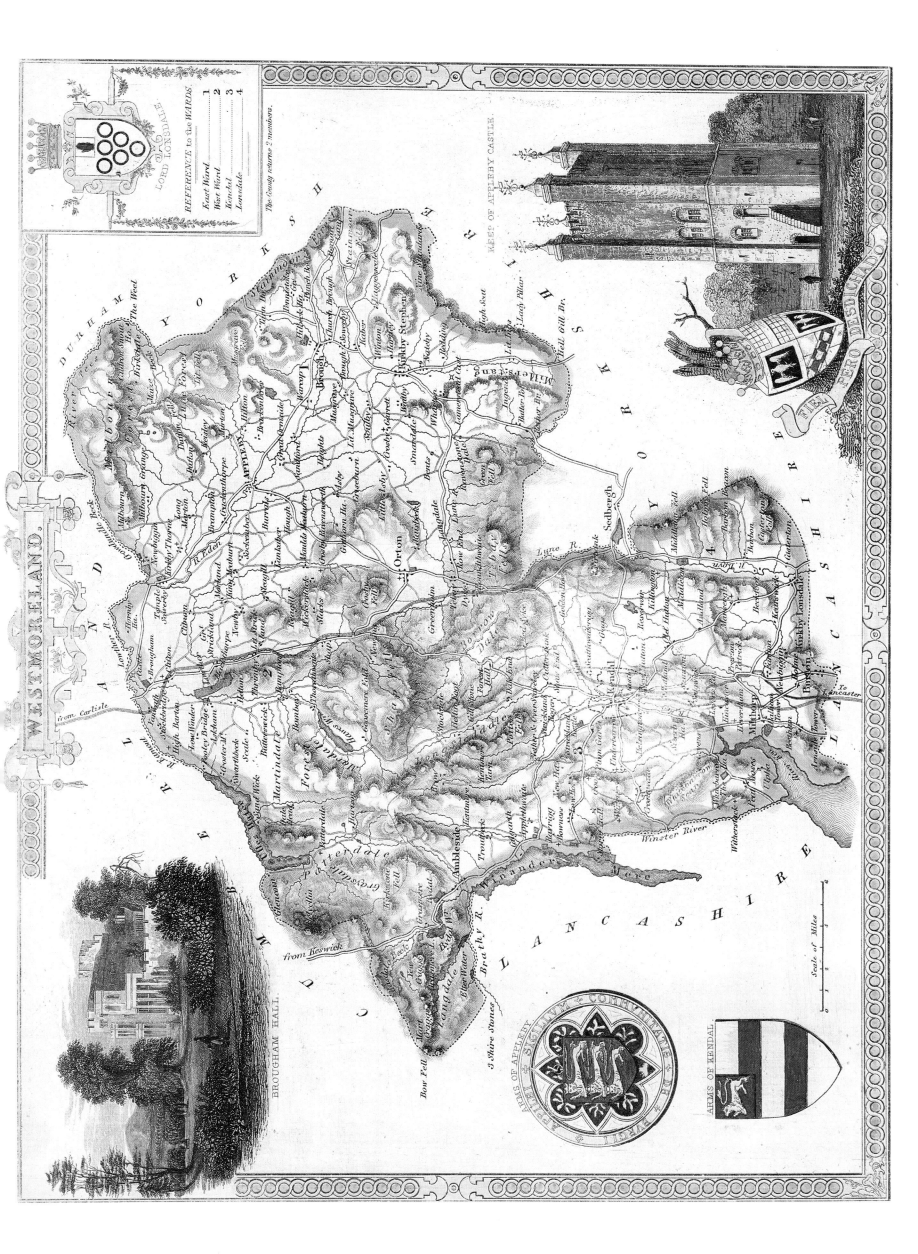

WESTMORELAND.

KEEP OF APPLEBY CASTLE.

FIEL PERO DESDICHA

DURHAM

YORKSHIRE

CUMBERLAND

LANCASHIRE

YORKSHIRE

Stainmoor

APPLEBY

Orton

Bowdale
Dale

Kendal

Sedbergh

Lune R.

Borrow
Dale

Potterdale

Ambleside

Winster River

Mere

BRAVDO

from Carlisle

from Keswick

3 Shire Stones

Bow Fell

Brath R. Winander

To Lancaster

LANCASHIRE

Scale of Miles

BROUGHAM HALL.

ARMS OF APPLEBY · SIGILLVM COMMVNITATE DE · APPLEBY ·

ARMS OF KENDAL

Isle of Wight

An island belonging to Hampshire, England, and separated from it by a narrow channel, called the Solent Sea. It is about 20 miles long, and 12 broad. It is crossed by a range of chalk hills, none exceeding 700 feet in height; and has a rather high level on the south side, one point being above 800 feet in elevation, but on the north side is lower and more level. It has some most romantic scenery amongst its hills; and at the western extremity are those remarkable detached masses of chalk, called the Needles. It has a rich soil, and produces corn, &c. abundantly. The beauty of the scenery, and its agreeable climate, make it a favourite resort for invalids and pleasure-takers. To the geologist it offers some very remarkable studies. Cowes is its principal place of maritime trade, and Newport its chief town. Population, 42,550.

Cowes

A sea-port on the north coast of the Isle of Wight, divided by the river Meden, or Medina. It is a place of good trade, resorted to by merchant-ships waiting for convoy, passage-boats to and from Portsmouth, Southampton, &c., and the station of the packet, with the mail from the island to London. Population, 4987.

Newport

It is called in Latin, Medina, from whence the whole island, on the east and west sides of it, is called East and West Medina. It is situated almost in the centre of the island, on the river Cowes, (which falls 7 miles below it into the sea, and which is navigable up to the quay here for small vessels,) 91 miles from London. Markets, Wednesday and Saturday. Population, 3858.

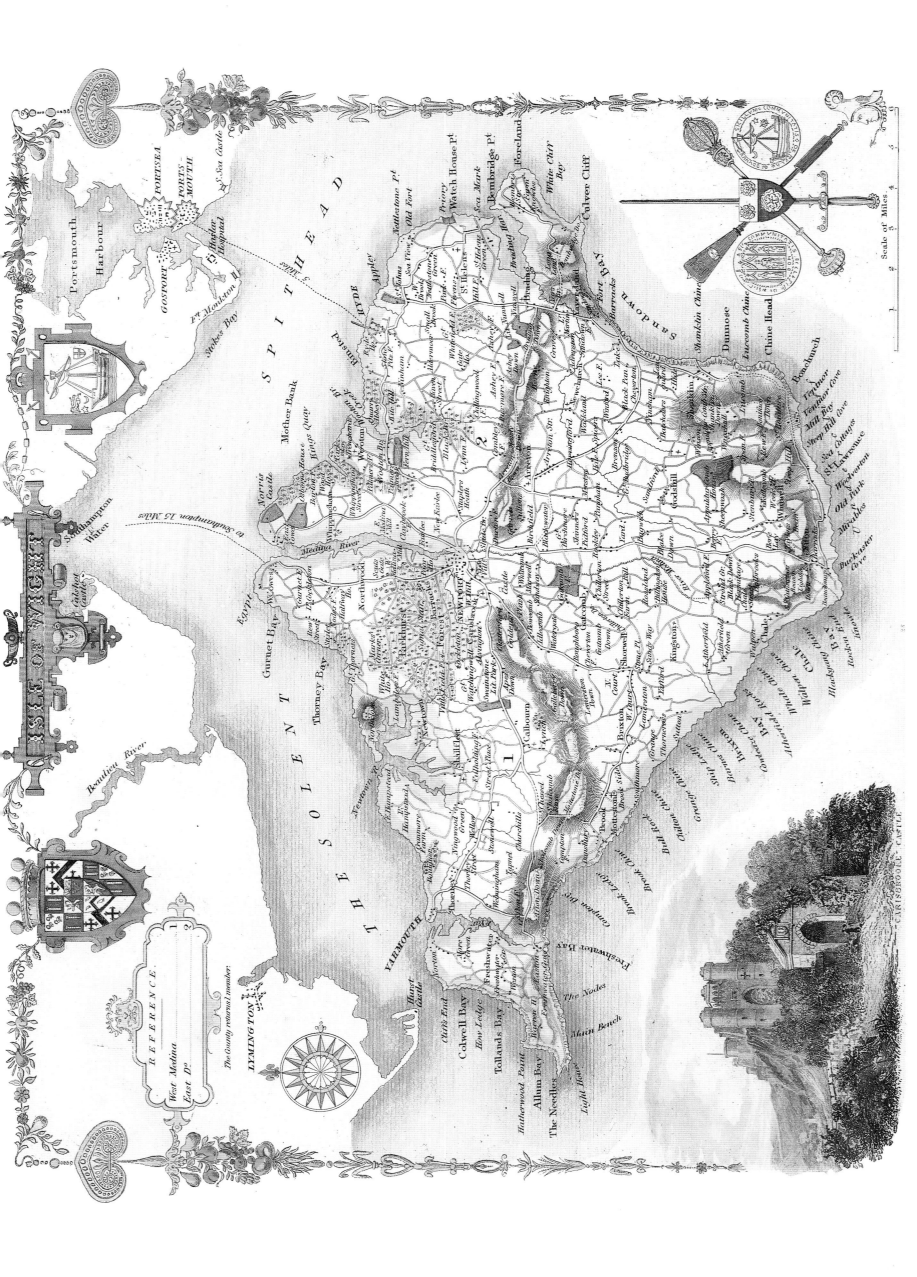

ISLE OF WIGHT

REFERENCE.

West Medina
East D°

The County returns 1 member.

CARISBROOKE CASTLE

Scale of Miles

Portsmouth Harbour

PORTSEA
PORTSMOUTH
GOSPORT
S? Sea Castle
Haslar Hospital
Ft Monkston
Stokes Bay

S   P   I   T   H   E   A   D

T   H   E   S   O   L   E   N   T

Southampton Water
Beaulieu River
to Southampton 15 Miles
Egypt
Medina River

Calshot Castle
Southampton Water

LYMINGTON

HYDE
Ryde
Binstead
Mother Bank
Norris Castle
Hings Quay
NEWPORT
Parkhurst
Forest
Carisbrooke Castle

Gurnet Bay
Thorney Bay
Newtown R.
SHALFLEET

YARMOUTH
Hurst Castle
Cliks End
Colwell Bay
How Ledge
Freshwater
Tollands Bay
Hatherwood Point
Alum Bay
The Needles
Light House
Main Bench
The Nodes
Freshwater Bay

BRIXTON BAY

Appley
St Johns
Nettlestone Pt
Priory
Watch House Pt
Sea Mark
Bembridge Pt
Foreland
White Cliff Bay
Culver Cliff

St Helens
Brading
Fort Bay
Barracks
SANDOWN BAY
Shanklin Chine
Dunnose
Luccomb Chine
Chine Head
Bonchurch
Ventnor
Steep Hill Cove
Sea Cottages
St Lawrence
Westverton
Old Park
Mirables
Buckaster Cove

Godshill
Appuldurcombe

Brook
Churchill

Wiltshire

An English county, bounded by Somersetshire, Gloucestershire, Berkshire, Hampshire, and Dorsetshire, being 54 miles in length, and 33 in breadth. It contains 304 parishes, and 21 market towns. The principal rivers are the Willey, the Adder, the two Avons, the Thames, the Kennet, &c. The air is generally good, though sharp upon the hills and downs in winter, but milder in the vales and bottoms. The northern part is hilly, and the south level, and the middle full of downs, intermixed with bottoms, wherein are rich meadows and corn-fields. There are several towns in it noted for the woollen manufacture. It abounds with relics of antiquity, the most interesting being ancient British earth-works, temples, tombs, &c. Salisbury is the principal town. Population, 258,733. It sends 18 members to parliament.

Salisbury

Salisbury or New Sarum is pleasantly situated on the river Avon, that waters most of the principal streets, which are large and spacious. It has several handsome buildings, particularly the cathedral, which is a stately, handsome building, with a lofty spire. Its chief trade arises from the silk manufacture. It is 80 miles from London. Markets, Tuesday and Saturday. Population, 10,086.

Stonehenge

The name of the most remarkable Druidical ruin of Great Britain. It is situated on Salisbury Plain, about 6 miles from Salisbury. It stands on the summit of a gently rising hill, and consists of a vast circular entrenchment, above 100 yards in diameter, in the centre of which is a great accumulation of huge masses of rock, some standing upright, and having other pieces laid transversely across them, but mostly prostrate; yet showing, in spite of this disorder, very clearly, that they are the relics of a temple, which consisted of a double circle of upright stones, the outermost being by far the largest, and connected by the transverse pieces into one continuous circular enclosure. Within the smaller circle, were five pairs of upright stones, with transverse pieces connecting them in pairs, about 20 feet in height, and before the centre one was a flat stone which seems to have been the altar. Beside these, there are several others within the circles, or between them and the embankment, and the whole number of them is 97. Most of them are of the kind of stone called gray-weathers, and was evidently quarried in the neighbourhood. Legends in abundance remain respecting the use and the erection of these stones, and one is embodied in the common name it bears among the Welsh, the dance of the Giants. Antiquaries and mechanicians have vainly endeavoured to show how, with the rude engines of the ancient Britons, such enormous masses could be quarried, transported, and erected here.

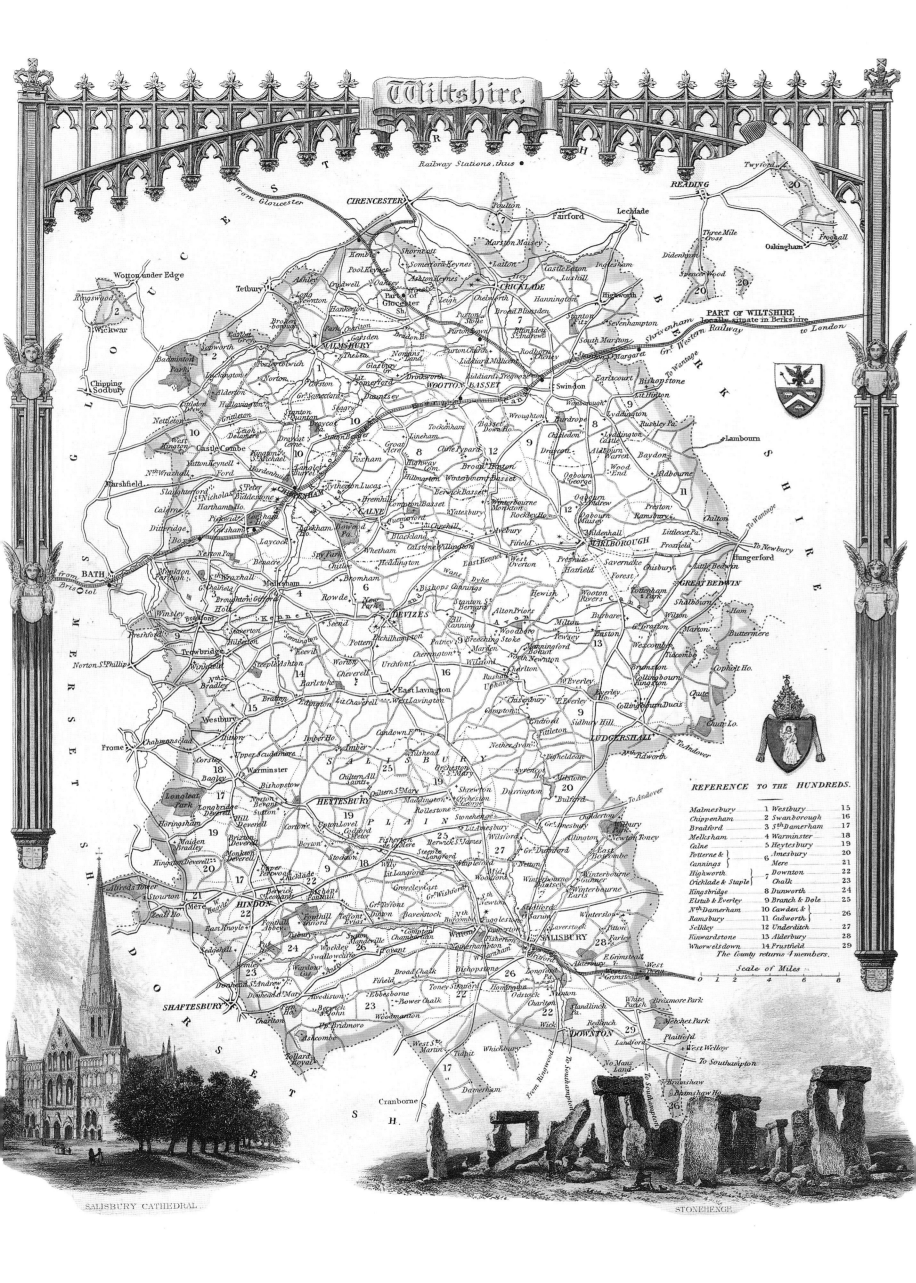

Wiltshire

SALISBURY CATHEDRAL

STONEHENGE

REFERENCE TO THE HUNDREDS.

Malmesbury	1	Westbury	15
Chippenham	2	Swanborough	16
Bradford	3	Sth Damerham	17
Melksham	4	Warminster	18
Calne	5	Heytesbury	19
Potterne & Cannings	6	Amesbury	20
		Mere	21
Highworth	7	Downton	22
Cricklade & Staple		Chalk	23
Kingsbridge	8	Dunworth	24
Elstub & Everley	9	Branch & Dole	25
Nth Damerham	10	Cawden & Cadworth	26
Ramsbury	11		
Selkley	12	Underditch	27
Kinwardstone	13	Alderbury	28
Whorwelsdown	14	Frustfield	29

The County returns 4 members.

Scale of Miles

Worcestershire

An English county, bounded by Warwickshire, Gloucestershire, Herefordshire, Staffordshire, and Shropshire; being about 35 miles in length, and 30 in breadth. It contains 152 parishes, and 12 market towns. Some parts are hilly, but it is generally level. The principal rivers are the Severn, the Avon, the Salwarp, the Teem, and the Stour. The air is very healthy, and the soil in the vales and meadows very rich, producing corn and pasture; while several of the hills feed large flocks of sheep. The chief commodities of this county are corn, hops, wool, cloth, cheese, cider, perry, and very fine salt. It has manufactories for pottery, iron, glass, &c. and a good trade by canals, &c. The chief town is Worcester. Population, 233,336. It sends 12 members to parliament.

WORCESTER

It is seated on the river Severn, over which is a beautiful stone bridge. The principal manufactures are of horse-hair cloth, broad cloth, gloves, and elegant china ware. Here are 9 parish churches, 3 grammar-schools, 7 hospitals, an infirmary, a water-house, and a well-contrived quay. It is 111 miles from London. Markets, Monday, Wednesday, and Friday; and a considerable hop market on Saturday. Fairs on the eve of Palm Sunday, the Saturday after Easter, August 15th, and September 19th. Population 26,306.

SEVERN

One of the largest rivers in England. It springs from Plinlimmon in Montgomeryshire; and after a course of about 200 miles through the counties of Montgomery, Salop, Worcester, and Gloucester, falls into the Bristol Channel. The Avon and the Wye are its chief tributaries. At its junction with the narrow sea it is about 2 miles across. It is the channel of a considerable trade, which is much increased by the canals. It is subject to the remarkable tidal phænomenon called the Bore.

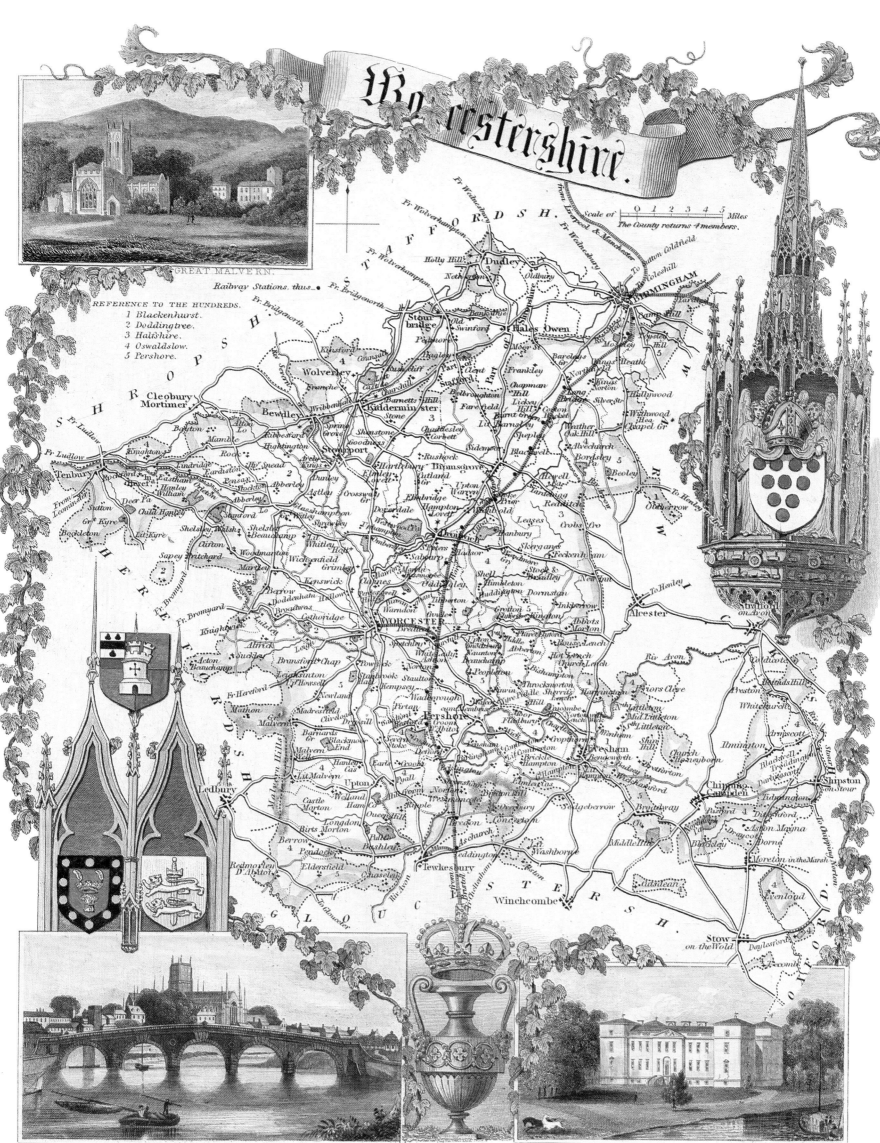

Worcestershire.

GREAT MALVERN.

Railway Stations, thus▬

REFERENCE TO THE HUNDREDS.
1 Blackenhurst.
2 Doddingtree.
3 Halfshire.
4 Oswaldslow.
5 Pershore.

Scale of 0 1 2 3 4 5 Miles
The County returns 4 members.

WORCESTER.

CROOM COURT.

Yorkshire: North Riding

The largest county of England. It lies on the North Sea, and is bounded by the counties of Durham, Westmoreland, Lancaster, Chester, Derby, Nottingham, and Lincoln. It is about 120 miles in its greatest length, and 90 in its extreme breadth. It consists of two highlands, divided from each other by the Ouse and its tributaries. That on the west of the Ouse valley has heights of from 2000 to nearly 3000 feet above the sea. The other is of a lower elevation, but its sea-cliffs are lofty and steep, and inland it is sometimes above 1000 feet above the sea. The rivers are the Ouse, the Swale, the Wharfe, the Derwent, the Aire, the Don, the Humber, &c. Coal, iron, building and lime-stone, &c &c. are found abundantly. It is very fertile, and produces in great plenty corn of all kinds; and there are excellent pastures, where cattle, sheep, horses, &c. are reared in abundance. Its manufactures are various and most valuable; the iron-works are numerous, and all kinds of cutlery and hardware, all kinds of cloth, woollen and cotton goods, silks, &c. &c. are made in vast quantities. The trade of this extensive and populous district is carried on by means of numerous canals and railways, communicating with all parts of the kingdom, and by the port of Hull, on the Humber, with foreign parts. York is its capital city, but there are many other places of great importance. It is divided into three parts, called the North, West, and East Ridings; and another smaller division is the ainsty of the city of York. Population of North Riding, 204,122, of West Riding, 1,154,101, of East Riding, 194,936; of the entire county, 1,591,480. It returns 37 members to parliament.

York

It is seated on the river Ouse, and is a large and beautiful city, adorned with many fine buildings, both public and private; containing about 30 parish churches and chapels, besides its cathedral or minster, which is a most magnificent structure. It is divided by the river into two parts, which are united by a stately stone bridge of five arches. The eastern part is most populous, the houses standing thicker, and the streets being narrower. It is surrounded by a strong wall, on which are many turrets, or watch-houses; and there are four gates and five posterns. It is a city, and the see of an archbishop. With its ainsty, or liberty, it constitutes a county. It is a place of considerable trade. It is 198 miles from London. Markets, Tuesday, Thursday, and Saturday. Population of city, 28,842; of city and ainsty, 38,320.

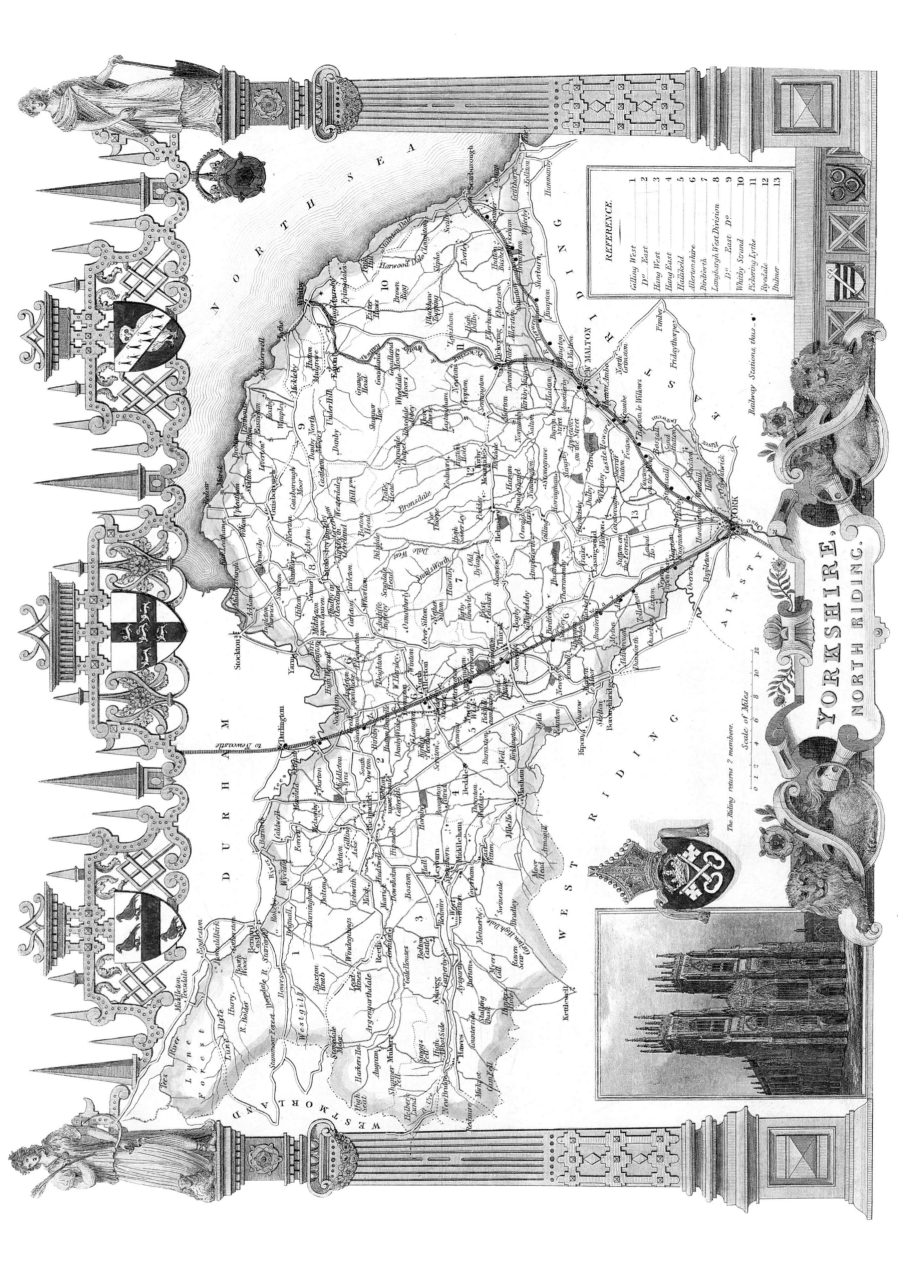

YORKSHIRE,
NORTH RIDING.

Railway Stations thus ⋯ •

The Riding returns 2 members.

Scale of Miles
0 1 2 5   10   12

West Riding

It is situated in a vale which trade has rendered one of the most populous spots in England. It is the principal of the clothing towns in Yorkshire, and is particularly the mart for the coloured and white broad cloths, of which vast quantities are sold in its magnificent cloth halls. That called the Mixed-cloth hall, is a building of considerable extent, in which the cloth is placed on benches, for sale, every market-day; and the whole business is transacted within little more than an hour, without the least noise or confusion, and with a whisper only, the laws of the market being observed here with particular strictness. The White-cloth hall, is a similar building. The manufactures that supply these two halls lie in the immediate vicinity of the town, on the banks of the rivers. Leeds has a manufactory of camlets, which has declined, and a flourishing one of carpets, resembling those of Wilts and Scotland. Here are also mills for the cutting of tobacco, and a great pottery, with several glass-houses. Within 3 miles of the town are numerous collieries. Of late years the town has been considerably enlarged; and some of the new parts are built, and building, in an elegant style. It is situated on the river Air, by which it communicates with the Grand Canal. It is 196 miles from London. markets, Tuesday and Saturday. Population, 88,741.

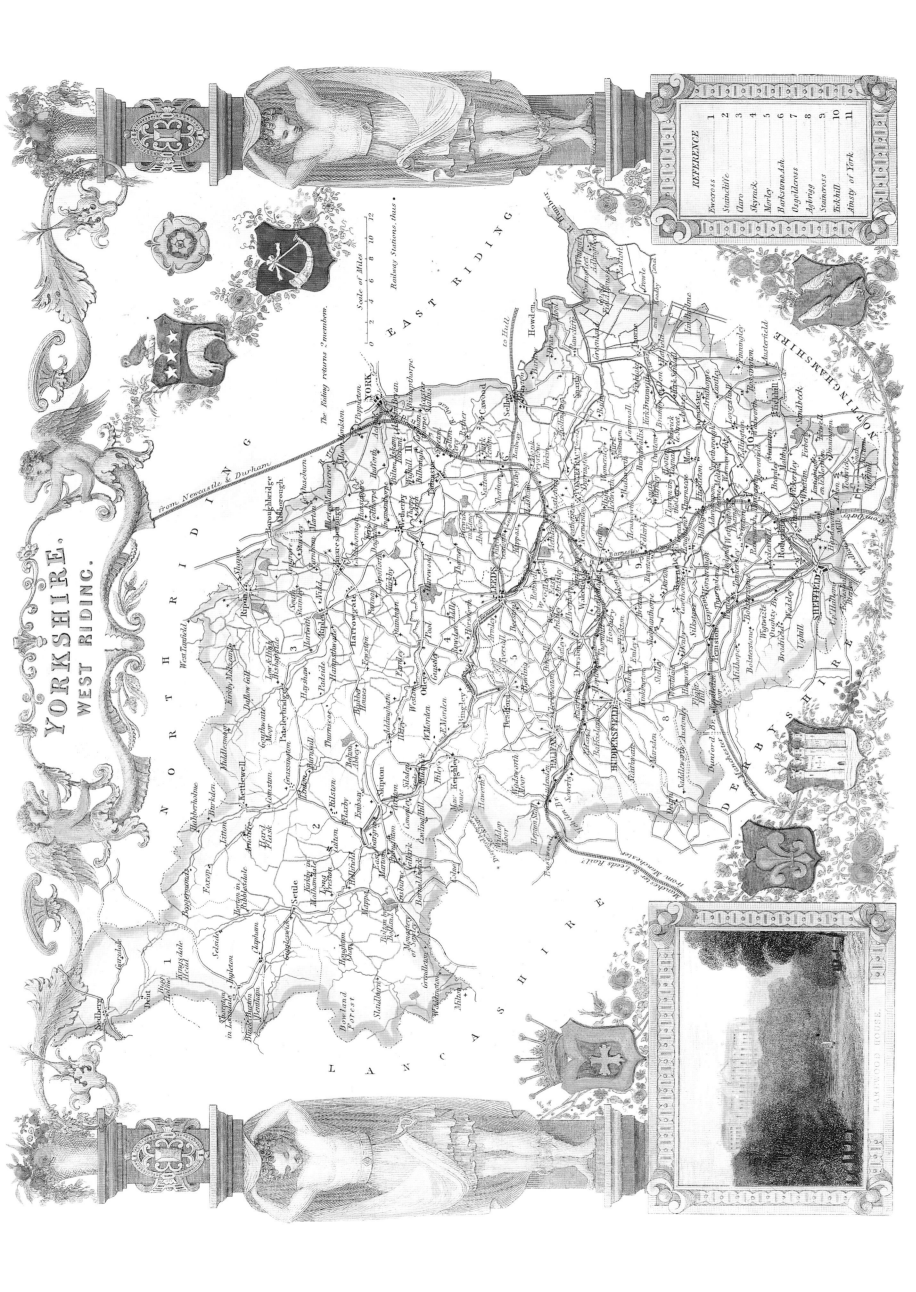

YORKSHIRE, WEST RIDING.

EAST RIDING

NORTH RIDING

LANCASHIRE

DERBYSHIRE

NOTTINGHAMSHIRE

Scale of Miles

The Riding returns 2 members.

Railway Stations, thus.

HAREWOOD HOUSE

East Riding

HULL

It is seated on a river called the Hull, which rises not far from Driffield, and here enters the river Humber. Its situation is extremely advantageous; for, besides its communication with the Yorkshire rivers and canals, it has access also, by the Humber, to the Trent, and all its branches and communications. Hence it has the import and export trade of many of the northern and midland counties. The foreign trade is chiefly to the Baltic; but it has also a regular traffic with the southern parts of Europe, and with America. More ships are sent hence to Greenland, than from any other port, that of London excepted. The coasting trade, also, for coal, corn, wool, manufactured goods, &c. is very extensive. The harbour is chiefly artificial, consisting of a dock, the largest in the kingdom, with which the river communicates, and in which 800 ships may ride safely and conveniently. Among the public buildings are the Trinity House, for the relief of seamen and their widows; an exchange; and a town hall. The grand stone bridge over the river to Holderness consists of 14 arches. It is 173 miles from London. Markets, Tuesday and Saturday. Population, 41,629.

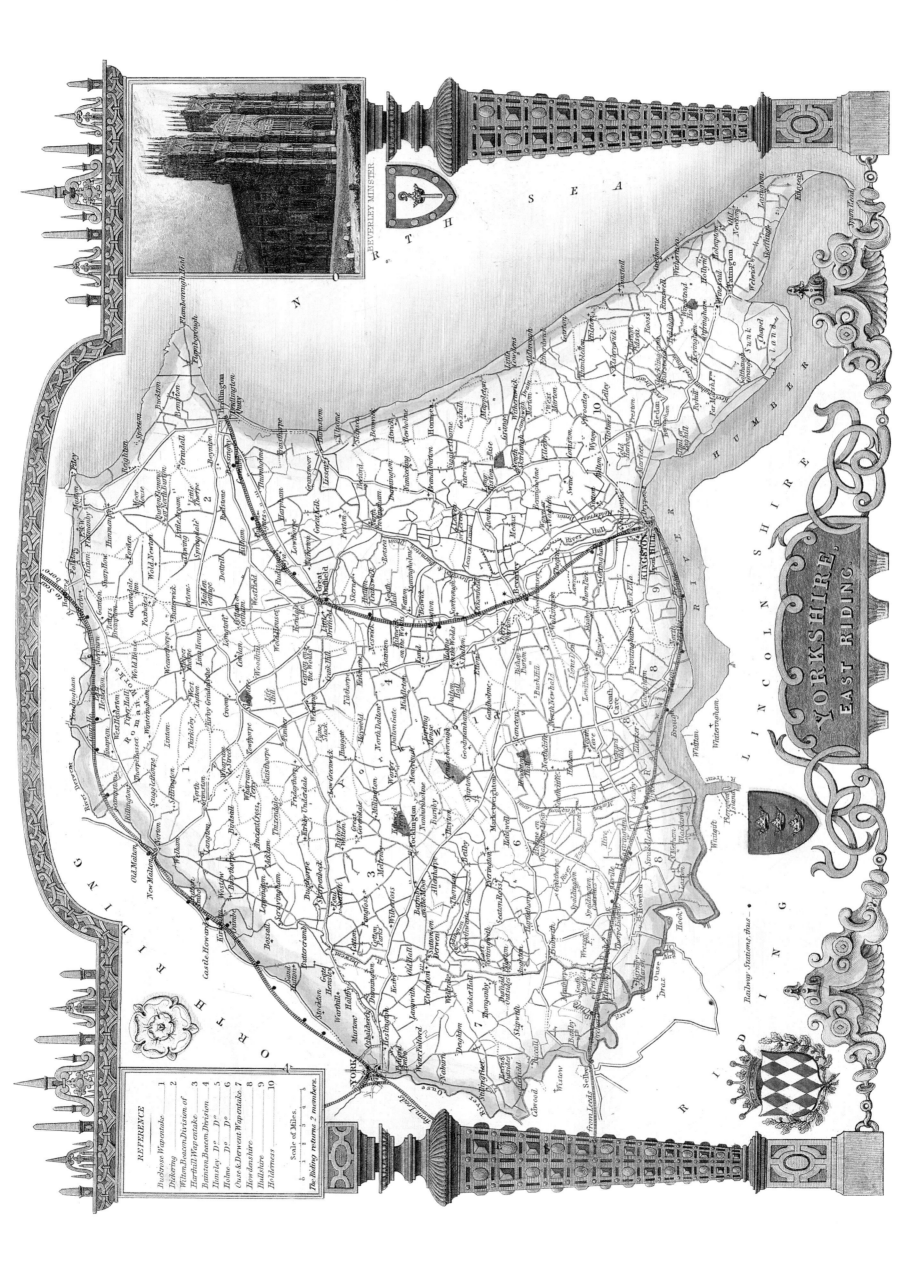

YORKSHIRE, EAST RIDING.

BEVERLEY MINSTER.

NORTH SEA

NORTH RIDING

LINCOLNSHIRE

RIVER HUMBER

KINGSTON upon HULL

REFERENCE
Buckrose Wapentake............1
Dickering...............................2
Wilton Beacon Division of......3
Harthill Wapentake.................4
Bainton Beacon Division.........5
Hansley. D.º   D.º.................6
Holme. D.º   D.º...................7
Ouse & Derwent Wapentake....8
Howdenshire..........................9
Hullshire.............................10

Scale of Miles.

The Riding returns 2 members.

Railway Stations thus ....